GRANDAD DASTARDLY

50 MORE FAMILY HISTORY TRAPS

Kate Broad & Toni Neobard

The Family History Partnership

Published by
The Family History Partnership
57 Bury New Road,
Ramsbottom, Bury
Lancashire BL0 0BZ

First published 2014

ISBN: 978 1 906280 47 5

Printed and bound by
Berforts Information Press
Southfield Road, Eynsham
Oxford OX29 4JB

What they said about our first book

Granny Was A Brothel Keeper
50 Family History Traps

"This little gem of a book . . . I am sure many family historians would find it invaluable, straight to the crux of the issue with its advice and easy to navigate . . . Worth every penny!"
Society of Genealogists

"Warm, funny and useful" *Family Tree Magazine*

". . . a great, lively book that manages to be as entertaining as the title suggests while packed with useful advice on conducting family history research." *Your Family Tree Magazine*

"The anecdotes are worth reading for themselves. Not only do they entertain, they cause us to reflect on and to reconsider our own assumptions." Catriona Williamson,
Who Do You Think You Are Magazine

"For those starting out on their genealogical voyage of discovery, it will be a valuable guidebook with a friendly, non-academic approach that has been rather lacking from family history bookshelves." Mike Paice, *Liverpool Family Historian*

" . . . but what makes it stand out from other family history books are the numerous real-life examples that bring the key points to life." *Oxfordshire Family Historian*

CONTENTS

GRANDAD DID A DASTARDLY DEED

Introduction by Toni Neobard

Welcome to our second family history book. In our first book," Granny was a Brothel Keeper: 50 Family History Traps", we tried to cover many of the areas which a newcomer to the hobby would need to know, as well as bringing fresh tips and hints to more experienced genealogists. We were delighted with the response we received. We weren't sure whether our humorous and, some might say, quirky approach to tracing one's ancestors was somewhat unique and might not have widespread appeal. However it seems that it was not a deterrent, rather the opposite. The idea that we may have put a smile onto the faces of so many fellow family historians gives us a warm glow. The positive feedback "Granny" has received has spurred us on to complete "Grandad", this second work.

This volume takes the story further, aimed at helping the reader get the best from the Internet; making the most of visits to archives; breaking down brick walls; and how to present your findings effectively, amongst other things. We've maintained our light-hearted, easy to read approach, using cartoons and stories to illustrate through-out, and showing just how interesting and bizarre the world of family history can be. Underlying this is sound knowledge built on our combined 45 years + of family history research. The majority of our stories and examples are true, and they seek to demonstrate that even the most experienced family historian can make a complete mess-up along the way. The words 'been there, done it' can be applied in full to us.

Writing the first book together was a challenge, as you never really know how you will work together, even if you have been friends for a very long time. After the success of the first book, we knew that we can work together, and this gave us confidence to embark on this second one with enthusiasm. I can't in all honesty say that every moment of writing together was harmonious, but we have made each other laugh a lot and at the end of the process are still friends.

We thank everyone who has taken the time to review our first publication. Thanks also go to those people who helped us get this second book ready for publication including Colin Piggott; James Ditton; Rob Cole; Jackie Ford; Tim Neobard; and Bill Neobard.

We'd also like to thank the following people who have let us use their family stories: Tom & Carolyn Hodder; Helen Davies; Sid Michell; Trevor Barlow; Tony Acott; Stephen Martin; Betty Hitchcock; Maureen Glanville; Gary Cremer; Kathy Rose; and Richard Pryor on behalf of his late beautiful wife Lisa.

And last, but not least, a huge thank you to Jim Wilkins who once again has taken our ideas and illustrated them to brilliant effect.

So what is next....perhaps "Auntie Was A Chicken Rustler...." or "Uncle Was A Knicker Nicker...."? Well maybe not. In any case, we hope you like this book.

✳✳✳

As in our previous book, we have tried to avoid using abbreviations where possible as we find them generally annoying. But there are a few places where we had to use them to avoid being long-winded and repetitive.

BMD: Births, Marriages & Deaths

DNA: Deoxyribonucleic acid (The Wikipedia definition for this is 'a molecule that encodes the genetic instructions used in the development and functioning of all known living organisms').

LDS: Church of Jesus Christ of Latter-day Saints (who provide a great deal of genealogical material to the public, both on-line and through their Family Search Centres).

TNA: The National Archives (this one is especially annoying as you have to say 'the TNA' so you are effectively saying 'the' twice, but this is the standard abbreviation).

URL: Uniform Resource Locator (but is a term used to refer to a unique name for a website or file address)

WW1: The First World War (1914 – 1918)

WW2: The Second World War (1939 – 1945)

WEB OF DECEIT

Using and getting the best from the Internet

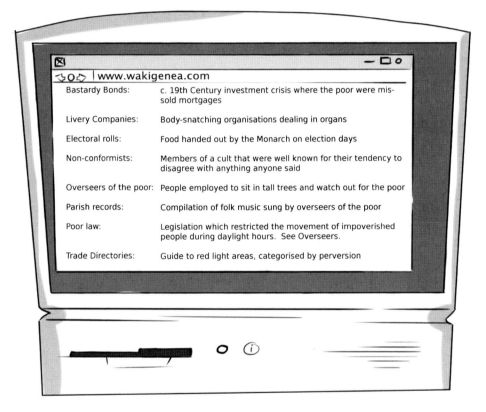

www.wakigenea.com	
Bastardy Bonds:	c. 19th Century investment crisis where the poor were mis-sold mortgages
Livery Companies:	Body-snatching organisations dealing in organs
Electoral rolls:	Food handed out by the Monarch on election days
Non-conformists:	Members of a cult that were well known for their tendency to disagree with anything anyone said
Overseers of the poor:	People employed to sit in tall trees and watch out for the poor
Parish records:	Compilation of folk music sung by overseers of the poor
Poor law:	Legislation which restricted the movement of impoverished people during daylight hours. See Overseers.
Trade Directories:	Guide to red light areas, categorised by perversion

The dangers of public submitted encyclopaedia entries

Trap 1. You think the Internet is always your friend

The Internet is an amazing thing, and it is likely to be an integral part of your family history journey. You can do lots of useful things on the world wide web, such as your grocery shopping; completing your tax return; join the search for extra-terrestrial intelligence; arrange for the artificial insemination of your prize Hereford cow, or marry a 22-year old Russian virgin (who of course loves you for your 58 year-old brain and not the size of your bank balance).

The capacity for computer-based mishaps (and downright lies) is, however, great. Toni recalls a time when on-line grocery was in its infancy, and she had made a fairly standard order with a well-known supermarket chain. To her surprise, on delivery she found that her order of 1 tube of toothpaste had multiplied to 18; she also received 12 bottles of ketchup; 1 dozen packs of 12 chocolate biscuit bars and 1 tin of cat food (2 dozen having been requested). The software concerned had presumably had a wobbly moment, and it is unlikely there was an attempt to trick Toni into buying 18 tubes of toothpaste! On the other hand, the intentions of the above-mentioned Russian lady looking for marriage may not be so innocent, and she is probably not as 'intact' as suggested. Additionally she may even turn out not to be of the female persuasion, but on the upside 'she' may be a welcome addition to the local shotputting team, and could provide a bit of colour on your family tree, too.

The need to exercise caution in your internet dealings extends to your family history hobby and it is wise not to take everything you find at face value. There is a lot to be said for maximising the amount of research you do on your computer from the comfort of your own home. For instance, it may save you having to pay out for expensive travel to archives, or spending hours in a traffic jam on the M25. You also have immediate access to food, drink and toilets and if you get something wrong you can swear like a navvy and no one will look disapprovingly at you. There is now such a wealth of information available to you at the touch of a few buttons, that it seems incredible to think that a few years ago to get access to the same information may have meant long journeys and days spent in record offices poring over old documents.

The Internet has a major drawback, which is that anyone can devise a website and put information out there.   Many excellent websites exist where the owners have shared their carefully researched and accurate family histories, and these can be very helpful. However, there are other websites which are based not so much on fact or research, but on the author's opinion or belief. Hence the importance of verifying what you have found before incorporating it into your family tree.

Because of the lack of quality control for web entries, you could be browsing materials that are complete fabrications or just stuffed with errors. This can be seen where people using social networking sites have drawn up profiles of themselves that have details that can only be described as dubious, even falsely claiming people as family members when they are simply just friends. When you see a description of someone you were at school with, who struggled to leave with any qualifications and who gives his day-job as a pilot for a major international airline (and his evening job as playboy), you have to wonder a bit. Especially as the last time you saw him, he was working as a bingo caller.

It is sometimes quite understandable that people might want to amend published details about themselves to show themselves in a better light. In 2012, several national newspapers reported that there had been an estimated 10,000 changes to MP's Wikipedia entries, to remove information that was untruthful, misleading or downright rude about each other. This editing was allegedly carried out by the politicians themselves or their staff, and it was reported that in particular, many references to the mis-claiming of expenses were removed. However, you can hardly blame Ken Livingstone for wishing to get the somewhat malicious description of "Twatface" removed from his entry, if the reports are true.

Malicious postings are not limited to online encyclopaedias. There are people who haunt forums and message boards to post entries with the sole purpose to upset or provoke other users into arguments. These posts may be abusive, provocative or take the form of naïve questioning. Such activity is known as 'trolling', and the people carrying it out as 'trolls'. Others forum users can be drawn into lengthy communication with successful trolls. An example of trolling is the person who argued that tornados do not exist, and any film purporting to show a tornado was part of a Government-led conspiracy. Not surprisingly, this would not have gone down well with anyone who had had their roof removed by an unfortunately-placed twister. Fortunately trolls are relatively few on genealogy-related forums, and if they do occur, generally the administrators of the forum will get them removed quickly, once alerted to their existence.

Kate's comment: There have been occasions where someone has posted what looks like a promising link to information you could use, but if you click on the link you could be downloading malware onto your system. Just because someone is posting onto a genealogical forum or website, this doesn't mean they are automatically well meaning!

Of course not all erroneous or unhelpful data is the result of deliberate sabotage. It is all too easy to make a genuine mistake, e.g. where there are two people with the same name in the same area and the researcher makes the link to the wrong one. People also like to make links because they enjoy the romanticism or kudos that may result, or because there is a story in the family which indicates such a link. If your surname happens to be Wren it would be easy to believe you could be related to a certain 17th Century architect, famous for building London's St Paul's Cathedral. This belief would be all the stronger if a family member had told you this was the case. However, just because someone shares a surname with a famous historical figure, or with an individual who appeared at a notable world event, this does not automatically mean there is a link. Only carrying out the research can confirm or deny this.

We wonder whether this will improve in the future with developments in technology, or will greater advances leave room for greater error? We can imagine a time when we can sit in our comfortable chairs and ask our intelligent computer to research our family history. Before you know it, you could be on the receiving end of an unexpected probe, where your DNA is extracted and analysed. After due thought, the results will be displayed direct to your smart glasses – but how disappointing would it be, if it turns out to be images of chimpanzees playing with sticks.

Trap 2. You trust other people's research

In days gone by, if there was something we wanted to know, we looked it up in a book. Nowadays we turn to the Internet as the go-to place for quick answers, rather than dusty old tomes. We have almost instant access to topics such as, for example, the children's TV show, Olimar the Wondercat or the 17th Century Earl of Aldbury. If you are interested in the Baldock Beer Disaster or have to find out about the Moroccans with Disabilities Act of 1992 for a research project, then Wikipedia is your place. Like all data on this site, the entries are public-submitted. Unlike most, however, all of those aforementioned topics were hoaxes, which in some cases were not discovered for many years before being identified and removed. The level of detail given for some of these is astounding – the Moroccans with Disabilities Act in particular ought to have received an award for its intricate and comprehensive nature. We are also sad that Olimar was not real, as we would have loved to have witnessed his ongoing struggles against his nemesis, Evil Derek the Dark Dalmatian.

Because of the generosity of fellow family historians, many family trees and associated researches are now published on-line. These may help you break through some of the brick walls in your studies. You can also get unexpected finds, such as a family document, story, or photographs which you are not likely to find in official documents.

Many people use Internet-published trees to trace their family roots back to the 17th and 18th centuries in a couple of hours, without having to leave their armchairs, or even change out of their pyjamas. Hopefully, such published information has been well researched, but it is always wise to confirm its accuracy. Once an on-line tree has a mistake, you may find that the same mistake crops up time and time again in other people's trees, simply because they have accepted the information on the original at face value.

Kate's comment: If we are going to use the Internet to buy something, whether a washing machine or a holiday, most of us, before parting with our cash, will spend some time researching the market, comparing prices and looking through product reviews. We like to see the opinions of others who have bought the product before us, and we put a lot of trust into such reviews, especially when there has been a consensus of opinion. However, when a family tree is posted on-line, there is generally no facility for family historians to comment on whether they have found the tree to be accurate or whether they disagree with the author's findings. So any information you find on that tree is unlikely to have been subject to any kind of peer review.

Similarly, photographs may be published with names attached which lead you to believe you are looking at an image of one of your ancestors. But how do you know those names are correct? Does the person who uploaded these images really know who they were or is it just their best guess? It might be a relief to establish out that the person resembling a bulldog eating a wasp, and labelled as your great-grandmother, is in fact Winston Churchill, and not your relative.

It is difficult to know why people publish wrong information. It may be through inexperience or mischievousness, or perhaps because people develop theories to explain evidence which does not readily knit together. Instead of keeping their theories to themselves, they instead present these as fact. For example, we were doing some research into a Danish man called Søren Pedersen, and we found some information about him on-line. It showed this man fathering dozens of children to different, concurrent wives. Rather than conclude that there could possibly be more than one Søren Pedersen around at that time, the researcher who published this had come to the conclusion that Søren was of a Mormon sect that practiced polygamy. This may have had something to do with the fact that the researcher lived in Salt Lake City, Utah, but he overlooked the fact that Søren had his children before the first Mormon missionaries arrived in Denmark.

Kate's comment: One thing to watch out for is sites that take information from published family trees and knits them together, using details which they have in common. These merges are done by computer and whilst they have the potential to be very useful, they can also be wildly inaccurate; a case of 1 + 1 = 42!

It can be particularly tempting to just go with what someone else has published, especially if the information they give shows details of an exotic or noteworthy nature. Toni has a story regarding her 8 x great grandfather, Abel King, which illustrates the problem:

"I was having a look around for information on this ancestor, and to my delight I found a family tree which showed Abel dying at sea in Indonesia in 1783. I then went on to find a further five published trees which gave exactly the same information. I was a bit surprised as I knew he was a Norfolk man, born and bred, but with so many people showing this information, I wondered whether there may be something to it. I knew he had been a fisherman so it was just plausible that he had joined a ship and sailed to foreign parts – maybe he had grown tired of life in a Norfolk village and wanted to explore the world.

"I went back and re-examined these family trees. Each author had cited one of the other tree authors as the source for this information – not one gave an original source of any kind, so they had all been copying each other. Presumably one of the tree authors had initiated the story but I couldn't pin down which one. So I decided to see if there was any truth to the story.

"My first area of research was the contemporary local papers, where I reasoned that such an unusual death would have been recorded. To my surprise I did find a report of Abel's death, dated 15th November 1783. It read: 'Monday one Abel KING, who lived at Hemsby, observing a smuggling cutter lay off the coast, went, in company with another person, on board, but some dispute arising between them and the crew, KING, we hear, by some accident, fell overboard and was drowned.

"Now this article was interesting enough in itself, but noteworthy is the distinct lack of the word 'Indonesia'. The article was published some four days after the drowning was reported as taking place. In the days before telephones or other speedy messaging services had been devised, it seems very unlikely that news of his death could have been received in Norfolk from Indonesia in just four days. So the evidence points to Abel's death occurring somewhere a bit nearer to home."

So a cautionary tale indeed about treating other's family history research with care. However, this does offer another tantalising mystery – what actually happened on board that boat? Was Abel King there to dissuade the smugglers from their illegal activities – or did he go on board to buy some cheap brandy for Christmas....

Toni's tip: There is no harm in regarding other people's trees as a potentially useful source of information. If you find something that you believe may be correct but can't prove it, make a note that it is unverified and try to establish it as fact at a later date.

Trap 3. You get the wrong subscription

Any hobby you take up is going to require some expenditure. Even if rambling in the countryside is your thing, you still have to pay out for appropriate footwear and maps. After all, you don't want to be up the wrong mountain in your carpet slippers. The deeper your involvement in your hobby, the more equipment you want to get and the more expensive this equipment becomes. Genealogy is no exception. Apart from all the equipment which can make your task easier and more efficient, the cost of on-line subscriptions can be quite draining on your finances.

But which subscription should you take out? Unfortunately no single on-line subscription site is going to give you access to all the records that may be useful to you. You could easily end up subscribing to a site that isn't the best for your circumstances or even paying out for two or three sites in your quest to get sufficient coverage. But don't let this put you off signing up. If you can afford it, a subscription to at least one of these would make your task a lot easier.

A subscription would mean that you could do a good deal of research from home. You wouldn't have the time constraints you would have if you had to travel to get the information. It also allows you maximum flexibility in your researching, in other words, allowing you to research as often as you like for as long as you like. However, if you don't have much time to research, and your hobby is very much an occasional one, you might never get full value for money out of your subscription. It might be better in terms of cost to go for some of the pay-per-view options, or taking a short-term subscription, e.g. for one month.

Even if money were no object, having a subscription to all the possible commercial family history websites would be overkill. The temptation to belong to all of them can be strong, especially as each strives to specialise in a particular area or field. Of course, many overlap, so if you subscribed to more than one, you could be paying for access to duplicate information. For example, a number have comprehensive transcriptions of Civil Registration Births, Marriages & Deaths (BMDs) indexes; or sets of census data.

As the quality of transcriptions, indexing and search facilities can be variable across different subscription sites, data which can't be readily located on one site may be more easily accessed on another. In this case it is a definite advantage to take out multiple subscriptions. However, in our experience this does not occur that often. Hence it may not be a strong reason to subscribe to more than one site, if funds are limited.

A useful consideration would be what the specialisms of each site are. Look to see how they link into your particular family circumstances. Did you have a lot of military men in your history or adventurous ancestors who were likely to appear on ships' passenger lists? Do you need access to foreign records? Does one site hold parish registers or transcripts for the places you are interested in? The answers may indicate that one site would be more worthwhile than another.

> **Toni's tip:** *Work out what might be your best subscription site or sites, and ask for contributions towards the cost of these as a birthday or Christmas present.*

As you become more experienced you may find that you are looking for a different record set e.g. newspaper archives; pure military records; or early records. That may be the time to cancel your automatic renewal on an existing subscription and explore some other on-line archive. However, you are unlikely to be able to find a subscription site specialising in your family's tendency towards bearded women – although there again, you might.

Trap 4. Your web searches don't go wide enough

At first, living on a desert island seemed like a touch of paradise to the yachtsman. After his boat had sunk, he swam to the shore and set about making a home for himself whilst awaiting rescue. He found a stream for his fresh water, driftwood to build a cabin; made fishing spears from flints and had a ready supply of coconuts from the palm trees fringing the beach. Twenty years later, it was somewhat less of a paradise. He was lonely, dressed in rags and down to his last three teeth. He longed for some company, clean clothes, a decent dentist and anything other than coconuts to eat. Somewhat of a pity, then, that he never bothered to climb the hill behind the beach. From the top of that he would have been able to see the town at the other end of the island, where he would have found friends, dentists aplenty, clothes shops and a three for two offer on mangoes that week. The moral of this story is that if you don't widen your web horizons you won't find all there is to find.

Compiling a family history requires the basic building blocks of birth, marriage and death records as well as census details. This will give you a solid but limited family history in terms of both number of generations back, and information about individual lives. So to expand it, and make it more interesting, you need to widen your searches. A review of what you have discovered so far may indicate your logical next steps and here are some ideas for information which can be found on-line:

- Wills & probate such as (pre-1858) held at the National Archives (TNA), or County Archives; or (post-1858) the National Probate Calendar;
- trade directories;
- occupational records (specialist archives);
- crime and punishment, such as Old Bailey on-line and transportation records;
- newspaper archives;
- burial records and memorial inscriptions, particularly military ones such as the Commonwealth War Graves Commission;
- military records;
- parish records – many online sources for these, e.g. Online Parish Clerks (OPC), or FreeReg,
- immigration and naturalisation
- village websites
- divorce indexes
- BMD certificate exchange sites.

There is so much information available, that we can't possibly list it all. So get to grips with your internet searching skills and get looking! Coverage is often patchy, but you can find some absolute gems.

You can draw on generalised information such as maps and photographs of the areas where your relatives lived (then and now), or descriptions of their working lives if they were involved in a particular occupation such as piano-making. You can compare contemporary and modern accounts of life in their place of origin, find out details of the churches they used, and maybe any involvement in nonconformist religions. Descriptions of military campaigns or ships your ancestors had links with can reveal fascinating details.

Kate's comment: I find it useful to use snipping tool software to cut out just the information I want from websites. This software allows me to paste together associated extracts into one document. This way I avoid having to wade through lots of irrelevant stuff and saves on printing costs if I want to create a paper copy. I save the source website addresses with the snips in case I need to revisit the original document for any reason.

A wider overview of your family history could be obtained by looking at other published family websites, trees and one-name studies. Surname meaning, derivation and distribution patterns may also be of interest. Being involved in blogs, forums and newsgroups can be useful, perhaps providing valuable leads.

No one knows everything that is out there and you will no doubt follow where your trail leads you. Researching the guidance notes and lists of on-line collections held at archives and libraries may bring to light something of relevance you hadn't thought of and will keep you up to date with changes.

> ***Toni's tip:*** *It will save you a lot of time if you get yourself a guide to genealogical sites on the Internet. Follow up with a subscription to a good family history magazine which will keep you up to date with new websites and changes to existing ones.*

Try also putting an ancestor's name into an Internet search engine. Sometimes all manner of interesting, intriguing or downright weird things can be unearthed. Searches are also worth repeating after a time since more and more information comes on line every day.

"It's not what you think, I was just doing an Internet search for great-uncle John Thomas Willey"

A number of websites are merely lists of links to genealogical resources. Whilst these sites can send you off in interesting directions, they can have their drawbacks. Often a link sounds very promising but clicking on it takes you to general information about the subject and not to the source document or index you may have hoped for. This can be frustrating and time consuming. Sometimes insufficient information is given on the link so you might dismiss it out of hand. Also some of these lists are phenomenally large, with up to a quarter of a million links. We have found it difficult to navigate these, so we tend to give them a miss, as there are usually easier ways to get to the same information.

Trap 5. Believing your search engine is all-knowing

Sir Timothy John Berners-Lee is the person credited with having conceived of a world-wide-web, and for getting it started, but it must be asked whether he ever really thought that it would take off in the way that it has. To mis-quote the late, great Douglas Adams: 'The web is BIG. You just won't believe how vastly, hugely, mind-bogglingly big it is.' It is getting increasingly difficult to find a subject that hasn't got at least one website dedicated to it, and in fact, some people consider finding just one a challenge. If you put a search into Google and get only one 'hit' this is known as a googlewhack, and believe it or not, some people do dedicate time trying to get one. Incidentally, if you want to try this yourself, search 'Googlewhack' – you will find several websites dedicated to the rules of this pastime!

So all this wealth of information out there is at your fingertips, right? Wrong! You might believe that your trusty search engine will wheedle out all the references you have searched for, but this is not the case. You may use only one of the many search engines, such as Google, and think that you stand a good chance of finding what you want, and often you will. However, estimates of how much of the Internet is indexed vary widely, with some reports suggesting that only 4% is indexed, and others saying 80%! What is established, however, is that if you use only one search engine, you could be missing out.

> ***Toni's tip:*** *Try different search engines to maximise your searches or those that consolidate results from a number of different ones.*

Most search engine indexing is done by the use of a clever system known as 'web spiders', 'web crawlers' or 'web robots.' These are automated programs that find pages and index them. Results will vary, as they are only as good as the people who programmed them. They work by following all links on a web page. Each page linked to will be analysed to see how it should be indexed, for example, by using words in the titles, headings, content or special fields known as 'meta tags.' It is possible to create a webpage which cannot be picked up by web spiders and thus avoids being indexed.

You may have already experienced the annoyance of finding a likely site on a search engine but when you click on it, after a wait, instead of the page coming up, you will get an error message. What this often means is that the Internet address has changed and whilst the information still exists in electronic form, the link your search engine had created has been broken. Luckily, there are a few things you can do.

Search engines generally save all or part of the source page (called a cache) as well as information about the web page. If you return to the results of your search, you may find a cache link associated with it. If that is there, click on it and it might take you to an old version of the page you want. The same result can be achieved by putting the word 'cache:' in front of the URL address, for example, cache: www.website.co.uk. If this does not work, then there are websites that store archived webpages. One such site is called 'Wayback Machine' - your search engine will locate this. If you enter the URL of the page you are interested in, this site will search to see if it is held in its archive.

If neither of these options brings you the site you wish to view, then don't give up. Try the search term at a later date, as indexes are updated regularly and you might get lucky. You might simply have to wait until the search engine's web spiders locate the site and index it again. Pity you can't do the same when you have misplaced your car keys.

Trap 6. You don't make the most of search engines

Now you have read the previous sections and decided you will have a go at a general search for your ancestor using a couple of different search engines. However, instead of a few valuable leads, up pops a load of drivel that has nothing whatsoever to do with your ancestor. A common result which particularly irritates us is where you put in your search terms, and you are asked if you have got the right spelling and get something else highly unhelpful suggested instead. So for instance, if you look up "Fred Jones Gimlet Maker" you are first asked if you mean "Fred Jones Omlet Maker" and then offered the chance to buy a book on him. Whilst such a book might be a boon to our researches, we feel that one is unlikely to exist.

Kate's comment: I have ancestors whose surname was Keen. If I carry out a search by just typing in a forename such as Elizabeth, and the Keen surname, I get things like 'Elizabeth was keen to ...' or if a genealogical site pops up, it is in the form of a list of names such as 'Elizabeth Jones, Mary Kane, Frances Keen ....'. No use at all!

What you have done is given the search engine parameters that are too broad. It is doing its best to find relevant matches but you can make the process much more efficient by using commands in the search dialogue box which narrows the parameters considerably. These commands consist of various symbols and words which should help give you the results you are interested in.

At the time of writing the most used search engine in the world is Google, and therefore the suggestions below apply to that, but in many cases may be used for other search engines.

" " *phrase search.* This makes Google search for examples of two or more words within the speech marks to the exclusion of anything else. Useful for names e.g. if you entered the term: **Jacob Marley** you would get many instances of the two names appearing in the same document but if you put speech marks around "Jacob Marley" you would get instances of that name when both parts were together in a document.

- *terms you want to exclude.* Putting a minus sign before a word shows that you don't want results to include that word, e.g. if you searched the term: **jaguar – cars** you would not get references to Jaguar cars but to other uses of the word "jaguar". It can also be used to prevent instances of a site coming up, for example, if you searched for the term: **London convicts – old bailey** you should not get references to the Old Bailey site returned.

... **Number range.** This is useful if you are trying to track down an individual who was around over a given period of time, e.g. **the term: "Jacob Smith" 1771 ...1849** should restrict results to any Jacob Smiths who are referred to in conjunction with any numbers within the 1771 to 1849 range. Of course, you might end up with pages of Jacob Smiths and their telephone numbers!

site: *Search within a specific site.* This tells Google to search within a site you have told it, and no other. For example, if you entered the term: **shurety site:oldbaileyonline.org** you would get a search of all incidents of the name Shurety appearing on the Old Bailey website. You have to state the name of the website accurately otherwise this will not work.

~ *synonym search.* Use of the tilde sign (~) makes Google search for results that include synonyms, such as the term: **~genealogy** will give you genealogy sites as well as results for ancestry, family tree and so on.

* *Fill in the blanks.* An asterisk can be used as a whole word wild card, e.g. for a middle name. For example, if you search for the term: **"Alexander Bell"** that is what you will get; putting in the term: **"Alexander * Bell"** will give you any that has a middle name.

OR *Or command.* If you want to look under two or more keyword criteria, by linking these with an OR command, you force the website to give you results that include either of the terms. For example, typing in the term: **Premiership Football 2008 OR 2009** will only give you hits for Premiership Football in 2008 or 2009, or both 2008 and 2009. Note the OR has to be in capitals.

+ *search exactly as it is.* Using the plus sign before the keyword in the search box forces google to search exactly on the term as you have written it.

There are a few other things you could try. Putting less information into your search box can help, for example, entering the term: **weather birmingham** will get a better result than the term: **what is the weather like in birmingham.** If what you get does not fully reflect what you are after, then it will at least give you an indication of what additional search terms to add.

As well as using a minus sign as a way of eliminating areas from your searches, using a hyphen between two words indicates a strong link between them, e.g. the term: **weather-birmingham** may get you even better results. You have to ensure the two words do not have a space between them as well otherwise you will be putting the term: **weather – birmingham** and thus get results for the weather <u>without</u> those for Birmingham!

Kate's comment: if you find something of interest, such as an address for your ancestor, try feeding that information back into the search engine. Sometimes this can yield a surprising amount of useful information.

Be specific about what you want. Putting in a more descriptive, accurate representation of what you want is more effective, e.g. entering the term: **compulsory education historical** will probably get you what you want more easily than the term: **when did children go to school.** Be prepared to use alternative descriptive words if the first ones do not get you the results you anticipated, such as if one of your search words is bootmaker, try using boot maker; shoemaker; shoe maker or cordwainer. This may flush out some different results.

Toni's tip: A practical way of using these search commands would be when you are getting a lot of results which show things you do not want. To illustrate, if you have an ancestor who happens to share a name with someone currently famous, you might be able to eliminate many of the references to the famous person. If your ancestor was called, say, Wayne Rooney, you could exclude results that mention football by entering the search term: "Wayne Rooney" – football and hopefully most of the references to the sportsman would not appear.

Search engines are becoming more sophisticated and will anticipate what you might be searching for, so that when you start to type your search term, google will try to think for you and offer a number of suggested search parameters. You may wish to ignore these, as some suggestions can be very strange. Those that are funny or downright weird are described as whoogles, and there are sites dedicated to listing the best of these. To give an example of a whoogle, typing in the term: **where were g** gives you the options of: where were Gauls from; where were grammar (sic); where were Greek plays performed; where were Geoffrey Chaucer's pilgrims going. And we only wanted to know where gummy bears were invented . . .

Trap 7. You register for everything

During your researches, you are bound to come across websites that offer a tantalising glimpse into the riches held by them, access to which can be all yours, if only you register with the organisation. Tempted by the thought of all your family history queries being resolved by this lovely, comprehensive and friendly website, you register. Unfortunately not only does the site turn out to be very limited in what it actually can offer, but you are then stuck with cheery emails inviting you to feed back to the site your opinion of the new improved website layout (for which you do not have an opinion as you never noticed what the original layout looked like). You may also then be on the receiving end of a host of emails inviting you to the McFarrgle convention in Pennsylvania in October (guaranteed to be a great weekend for all the McFarrgle descendents, of which you are not one), or find yourself bombarded with 'spam' emails offering you a wide range of services, even though you have never expressed an interest in obtaining, for example, a 'legal high' or double-strength Viagra.

Once you have given your personal details to a site, you have no guarantee that your information will not be passed onto third parties, and often very little comeback if they do so. Any responsible site will offer you the option to 'opt out' of being contacted by 'carefully selected' third party organisations – the 'carefully selected' in this instance most likely means the ones who pay the most for the contact information. If you choose to 'opt out' this is generally respected by UK-based organisations but sometimes you cannot easily tell – if you have any doubts at all, don't use the site.

Of course, this is if you can just get away with a straightforward registration of just your name, telephone number and email address, even though there does not seem any obvious reason for giving out this information. Many sites will advertise that you can 'search for free' which of course you can. However, the search is as far as you will get as when you find something of interest you will need to register. It is at that point that you are presented with a requirement to give them your credit card details, so that for a modest fee (but in some cases, exorbitant) you can have a look at the original documents and so on. If you do decide to pay the registration fee, you might well find that they hold only one useful snippet of information and the cost of registration far exceeds the value of the site to you.

Kate's comment: *So many of us, when presented with 'Terms and Conditions' when registering on a site, or when shopping with a new company on-line, skip through the generally long and boring detail and just check the box which says 'Agree' to the terms and conditions set out. Although it is tedious, you should read them. You might come across something that you don't like. For example, I was buying something on-line recently and read the terms and conditions and found that had I agreed, I would have authorised the company to carry out credit checks on me for third party companies. There was no reason for this, I wasn't applying for credit so why would they want this information about my credit-worthiness? It was probably nothing more sinister than categorising my status in terms of marketing, but I cancelled the purchase anyway, I wasn't going to agree to that.*

If there is no registration fee to pay, the site may employ a 'pay per view' system which could be more reasonable if you only want to view a small amount of data. However, many people will quite correctly have concerns about giving personal details over the Internet, in case of credit card frauds, viruses and general intrusions onto your privacy. As a general rule, it is common sense to give the same personal information over the Internet as you would give to a complete stranger on a street corner – in other words – very little information indeed.

Apart from the risks outlined above, registration on a site generally means that you have to create a password to allow access to that site. Many sites now place quite stringent demands on passwords used, such as 'must be at least eight characters', 'must contain at least two numbers' and/or 'must contain a mix of lower and upper case letters'. Some sites even have a password test so they can inform you as to how secure or otherwise your password is. So either you use the same complicated password for every site or you create a different elaborate password for each site. Using the same password gives security problems – if someone finds out your password he/she will have access to all your password protected sites. Using a different one means remembering them all, and you probably wouldn't be surprised to learn that a huge proportion of people write down their passwords on a piece of paper which they keep next to their computer. There is no easy solution to this, but some people reserve complicated and unique passwords for more crucial sites, such as on-line banking, and draw from a pool of easier to remember passwords for less critical ones, like on-line forums.

So now that we have you feeling paranoid about any use of the Internet, what can you do to make use of registration-only sites? A useful tip is to use their 'free' search engines. Once you have found reference to a piece of data that might be of use, you now know that this data exists. Try searching other sites to see if this information is held elsewhere. The authors have had success with this technique on several occasions.

It goes without saying that you should always have up-to-date security software, which prevents not just virus infection but filters out any spyware programs that come your way. You could always, too, consider using false details if you are asked to register, but this may be ineffective. Many websites get round this by emailing confirmation of site access details to the email address given, so if this is false you won't be able to get on the site anyway.

Toni's tip: *If giving false information doesn't work, try setting up a new email address just for the purpose of these registrations. Many email accounts can be set up for free, e.g. a hotmail account, and if you are bombarded with spam on this account, at least it won't appear on your regular one.*

Trap 8. You don't do anything with what you find

There are people who claim to have a photographic memory, or more correctly speaking, an eidetic memory, whereby just studying an image for a short time enables the individual to recall the image in its entirety. Some experts believe that up to 10% of children do this naturally, although the percentage of adults capable of doing so is much less, probably around 1%. Other experts claim eidetic memory to be utter nonsense and it is simply training that can achieve such a feat. In all probability, then, if you were to read this page, you may recall the gist of it, but you wouldn't be likely to remember the whole page, verbatim.

So why is that, given that the vast majority of us will not remember details of something we have seen, when we come across something interesting on the Internet, we think to ourselves "I'll remember where I saw that," because we won't.

Dealing efficiently with any data found is the key to this. It is so easy to get caught up in the thrill of the chase but not deal with the more difficult task of piecing your information together. Toni has a story to illustrate:

> "I recently came across a record which shows a distant relative of mine to have served in the militia at the time of the American Revolution. I know I have seen a reference to someone of the same name being transported to America. I believe it is the same person but I need the transportation record to check the dates to confirm my theory. The problem is, I can't find that reference. I have gone through all my papers, including the 'consider later' pile. I can only think that although I saw the reference, I did not print out a copy and file in an appropriate folder for that family line."

When surfing at our computers we might come across a nugget of information which, although we cannot immediately link this to our family, we think there is a good chance there is a connection. At that point we would either save it somewhere or print off this exciting piece of information for later consideration. And there it will sit, along with all the other bits of interesting snippets of data we have collected, for one month, two months, six months, a year – because we don't ever really get round to looking in the 'consider later' collection.

Toni's tip: *If you are keeping a copy of information sourced from the Internet it is a good idea to associate the web address with it, so that you can always go back to the original if you need to.*

If you are a regular surfer, you may even find that you print off the same data several times as you had forgotten that you had seen something before and even have a copy sitting in your 'consider later' pile. Not only is this a waste of paper, ink and time, it also makes your pile somewhat larger than it needs to be, and who wants large piles?

Trap 9. This looks interesting – getting distracted

"John Young, reading Mathematics; Jack Mackintosh, reading Molecular Biology; Stephen Jobson, reading 19thC Gothic Literature; Catriona Biggs, reading Genealogy and Everything Else"

For the non-family historians out there, getting distracted whilst on the Web generally means getting a bit involved in a social networking site, or seeing what the weather has in store for us. Pity the poor genealogist, then, who sits down with every intention of spending a few moments looking up the first marriage of their great-great-grandfather (his second marriage being to your great-great- randmother), only to discover that the father of this spouse was a glassblower. How interesting – and that is where the problems start. For the next three hours, the genealogist will be researching glassblowing in the 19th Century and will become a minor expert in the subject. So even though this person has no direct genetic link to you, you have been distracted into finding out anything you can about his livelihood.

One of the most tempting areas you can have is on-line newspaper indexes. You can start by looking for a specific fact but end up being drawn into discovering the reasons behind the failure of the 1885 lentil harvest in Morocco or become an expert in 19th century gardening implements. This is fine if you have unlimited time, but if your time is precious then this is probably not the best way to spend it.

If you are not a person of strong will, whatever you do, don't look at the Old Bailey on-line site. This gives details, amongst other things, of trials which took place at that court. This is a fantastic resource and if you suspect you have ancestors of dubious morals, it is worth having a look. The authors have found ancestors on that site (for other people, not themselves, of course) who were murderers, horse thieves, ran brothels or committed fraud. But beware, there is so much on that site of interest to the curious person, you can get lost to the rest of the world for days.

Kate's comment: Just to illustrate this point, I went onto the Old Bailey site to check some details. Before I realised it, I was reading up on the Ordinary of Newgate, the Chaplain of Newgate prison, who gave spiritual care to prisoners who were condemned to death. He also had the right to publish the final speeches and crimes of these poor individuals. Fascinating stuff, and well worth a read, but it did somewhat distract from the task of writing this section!

It is very easy to be reading a page of useful information which includes an interesting link to another site. It may be tempting to follow that link as you might find more information of relevance, but before you know it you have navigated away from your original, useful page and then you will have to try to find your way back to it. So before clicking on that link, make sure you have made a note of the site you are on and the nature of the information on it, so that you can find your way back with ease.

Toni's tip: If you know you are of an easily distracted disposition, then perhaps you just need to accept your 'flaw' and allow yourself some time for additional reading. After all, if you are reading up on historical events then this can only help you get a better grasp on history in general, and for the genealogist, this can be very useful indeed.

Trap 10. Not knowing when to stop

Studies by educationalists and psychologists on individual attention spans generally agree that for young children, the maximum concentration on a task is around 5 minutes, rising to 20 minutes for adults. Some people will argue that a 20 minute time span for concentration is lessening due to the effect of television and computer games making people thirst for frequent changes of stimuli. We have come to the conclusion that such studies have never been carried out on people researching their family history, as in our experience it is quite possible to work solidly for several hours without a significant lessening in concentration.

Even if you are a very disciplined person and not subject to being distracted, it is still possible to get so engrossed in your researches that you become oblivious to the passing of time. When your significant other announces at 11 pm that he/she is off to bed, no doubt when you respond that you will be there in a minute, you mean it. Next time you become aware of your surroundings, it's 3 am and you are freezing cold because the central heating went off some four hours earlier. Sneaking into bed at that time in the morning, trying and probably failing not to wake your partner, does not tend to go down well. Even if you do manage not to wake him/her, sleep doesn't come easily as your brain is processing all that lovely information you have been collecting.

A significant cross-section of people, of course, will not recognise this scenario simply because they are larks, not night owls. In other words, they will be tucked up in bed whatever the circumstances by 9.30 at the latest, but at 5 in the morning they just have to go and check out a new theory which occurred to them as they awoke at 4.30. Their subconscious may register the presence of other family members as they get up, and they may even be able to automatically answer such queries as "have you seen any clean socks" or "I have had to take £20 out of your purse as I have run out of cash". Eventually the dog will give up any hope of being taken for a walk and will return to its basket, and it might occur to the larks around midday that they are hungry and also still in their pyjamas.

Toni's tip: *It is a good idea to set a reasonable cut-off time beyond which you will not work on the computer. This will benefit not just the quality of the work you are doing, but also help keep your joints from getting stiff through sitting too long in one place, and also possibly improve relations with the rest of your family! You could set an alarm clock or timer to go off after a suitable time. If you are half way through some interesting reading when this happens, make a note of the website address and the nature of the research you are interested in and return to it at a later date. Keep a record, too, of the sites you have visited already during that work period and the search criteria you have used, as you don't want to return to them again on a subsequent occasion if they proved to be of little use in the first place.*

WE SEEK HIM HERE, WE SEEK HIM THERE

Finding Ancestors in Other Places

Not only did it explain why we couldn't find great uncle Rupert's death entry, it also explained why the fire always smoked

Trap 11. Making assumptions about your ancestors

It is a commonly held view that, in the past, people remained in the area where they were born and held the same occupations throughout the generations – so a blacksmith's son would become a blacksmith and inherit his father's business, and so on. Whilst this did undoubtedly happen for many people and many generations, there are others for whom this was not a reality. Thomas Cromwell, for example, born around 1485 of humble origins, worked abroad as a soldier, merchant and accountant before becoming a lawyer, worked for Cardinal Wolsey, became an advisor to King Henry VIII, and finally rising to the rank of Earl of Essex before it all went a bit pear-shaped for him, when he was beheaded for treason in 1540. If you thought you had found an ancestor who described themselves as having such different occupations and ranks, you probably wouldn't believe you were dealing with just one person and would be very likely to dismiss the evidence before your eyes.

Kate's comment: I was recently looking into a friend's family history. She was convinced the male line could not be done as she was sure the family was from the Republic of Ireland – a place notorious for having very little by way of family records. This was her belief as the name, Shurety, sounds as if it is an Irish name and she had been told they were from Ireland. She was, therefore, quite surprised to find I could take her back to around the mid 1700's with the family living in Hampstead. In fact, there were no indications of an Irish connection whatsoever.

Toni's family on her father's side followed the classic industrial revolution migration path of country dwellers, upping sticks in the early to mid-nineteenth century and becoming economic migrants by moving to the East End of London. They were poor, often just having a room in shared accommodation. It was surprising therefore to discover in an early census that one of her great grandfathers had owned a pickle factory. They had servants and owned property. By researching further back in time it was found that they were from professional stock. So just where did that family fortune go? The answer lies with information gleaned from a distant relative. This great grandfather was a bit of a wastrel, and had gambled the family money away until there was nothing left. His daughter was left to take in

35

washing and mangling to make ends meet, although ironically she was considered relatively "well off" in their neighbourhood because she had a spare pair of sheets that she could pawn, and neighbours used to borrow them for this purpose.

Losing money through gambling was not the only way that fortunes can change. The rules of primogeniture established that the entirety of the estate was inherited by the oldest son of the family, with nothing left for the other children. This stopped any fortune being diluted amongst numerous siblings. Unless these other children managed to make a 'good' marriage where the spouse brought an income with them, they could quickly find themselves in much reduced circumstances.

We tend to think that official records can be relied upon to give an accurate picture of someone, but we can be misled. For example, we came across someone who was a farmer of several acres on one census, only to be shown as a general labourer on the next. So how could such a dramatic change in circumstances come about? In this case the reason for such a change was made clear by the wills of the individual's mother and step father. His mother had inherited the farm from her second husband, and her son from her first marriage had moved in with her and farmed the land. However, when the mother died the estate was distributed to her step children in accordance with her second husband's will and so the poor son had none.

Similarly, Toni found that the Neobard family gave every indication of being a fairly well-to-do lot. They appeared on censuses as having good occupations such as tailor or wine merchant, and a will from the 17th century showed the direct ancestor as being a yeoman farmer, someone who would have been quite comfortably off. It was a surprise to find that the Overseers of the Poor Accounts showed the family in regular weekly receipt of handouts. Her theory that they were working in good trades and thus were comfortably off had been completely overturned.

So the moral of this tale should be that it does not pay to make assumptions about your ancestors. Fortunes came and went very quickly and not everyone carried on the trade of their father. If your father was the village blacksmith who had five sons, it would be unlikely that the village could provide enough work if all the sons became blacksmiths, so the options for some would be either to find another trade, move to another part of the country or possibly do both.

Trap 12. You don't know where to look next

So you have gathered enough evidence that you have the bare bones of your family tree. You have consulted certificates and census returns and you know who your ancestors were, where they lived and what they did for a living. Ideally you will have married them off, found their children and ultimately buried them. But what more could you find out about them?

It helps if you concentrate on one individual on your family tree at a time. Try to find out answers to these major questions - what did they do, where did they live, what happened to them during their lives? At this point, go back to any family papers, diaries and letters for further clues. It will help you if you think in detail of each aspect in turn:

Occupation
Think about what you already know about them. What records exist about their occupation? If they had their own business they may appear in local business directories or might have advertised in local newspapers.   If they worked for a large organisation such as the post office; a railway company; a county police force; or a large manufacturing company, staff records for the period in question may survive. If there are no relevant staff records, an alternative source of information might be newspapers, as they may carry reports about the companies and sometimes announce retirements or long service celebrations. Think about activities which may be related, for example, a fisherman might also have served as a lifeboatman or been in the Naval Reserve.

Where they lived
Addresses for your ancestor can be found, for example, on census returns, certificates and parish records. It is worth looking for these addresses on contemporary maps to see if they still exist. You might find information about the history, type of street and events which occurred there, either on-line or in local libraries. There could be photographs or drawings which are contemporary to when your ancestor lived there. If the address still exists you could pay a visit and look at the house where they lived or find an image of it on-line. A visit to the area might surprise you with information such as a memorial plaque in the parish church or even a street called after your

ancestor! Local libraries might have oral histories which can give you an insight into the lives of your forebear.

If he lived in London you might find his street on the Booth Poverty Map which would give you an idea of the people living on his street and how wealthy or poor they were likely to be. Earlier ancestors might appear on the Hearth Tax rolls which would enable you to judge their wealth by the number of hearths they declared.

Early lives

Before 1881 some children, especially those from more affluent families, received some schooling and records of this may exist. Schooling was compulsory for everyone after 1881 so if you know where your ancestor lived as a child you may be able to establish which school he or she went to. There may be Admissions & Leavers registers and Headteachers' log books that have survived that show evidence of school attendance.

Lives as adults

Did your ancestor serve in the army? Most surviving army records, up to and including WW1 (First World War), are available on-line through subscription, or at the TNA at Kew. If they served after WW1, direct descendants can apply for service records for their ancestors from the Ministry of Defence. Service records can be fascinating, as you can find out information such as a physical description of your ancestor, including height, eye and hair colour, or distinguishing marks such as tattoos, as well as details of next of kin. Medical details are often shown, and you can discover unexpected details about your great-grandfather, such as that he acquired a venereal disease during a tour overseas. If your family hold medals from your ancestor from WW1, these have the name and army number of each recipient which helps you identify the correct service record.

Kate's comment: My father tells a story of when he was in the Navy during WW2. Shore leave in various ports often mysteriously coincided with outbreaks of symptoms not best discussed in polite society. This meant the sailor thus afflicted needed to pay a trip to the 'special clinic'. This place was colloquially known as "Rose Cottage". Even to this day my Dad cannot pass a twee country residence bearing that name without smirking!

Could your ancestor have been a criminal, a victim of crime or a witness to a crime? Gaol records and newspaper reports may indicate this as a possibility, sometimes with surprising results. Toni once carried out a speculative on-line newspaper search for a client's ancestor, using just his name and the village he came from. This revealed that his wife had once taken him to Court on a charge of assault. He had accused her of boiling his sausage dumpling dinner in his dirty painters' apron, something which she emphatically denied. He threw the offending meal at her and was convicted on that charge. It was probably not the dumpling that sealed his guilt, but the fact that he landed a punch on her nose at the same time.

Your ancestor may have had a noteworthy hobby or pastime, for example, he might have been an accomplished sportsman or musician. Family stories might refer to an ancestor as a long distance runner, and you might find out that he competed for his county and there could be reports in the local newspaper about this. Alternatively he might have been active in a trade union or campaigned on local issues.

19th and 20th century ancestors may at some stage have had a photograph taken of them. These are worth studying as there may be clues to follow. For example, wearing of uniforms might indicate military service and an army cap badge could identify the regiment. Other uniforms might indicate occupations such as railway workers. Group photographs might indicate a church outing, union meeting, works outing or a major family event. The clothing worn will often give a clue as to their social status and wealth, as well as dating the photograph.

Consider consulting poor law records, particularly those detailing workhouse admission and discharge and poor relief, even if you think your ancestor was well-off and not likely to need these services. Wealthy ancestors might have given funds towards helping the poor. Where information is scarce, especially for those early ancestors, you could research the conditions they may have lived in, what they may have eaten and how they may have dressed.

Lastly, it is worth considering the death of your ancestor. Do you know when and where they died and the circumstances around it? People did not always die peacefully in their beds - they may have died in a workhouse infirmary; a house fire; a railway accident; been run over by a horse and cart or even drowned at sea! Their death might have been newsworthy so again a look at newspaper indexes might find something interesting. Did your ancestor leave a will? Do you know where they were buried, and whether they have a gravestone, tomb or memorial plaque?

Nowadays, with the advent of social networking on Internet sites, there is much more recorded about the daily lives of individuals than ever before. It is questionable how valuable this would be to family historians in the future if all this information was available to them. Would the genealogist in the year 2118 really want to know that his great-grandmother Kylie Bennett ate spaghetti bolognaise for her tea on 25th February 2016?

"My brother George has written to say he had duck breast and peas for dinner. I am replying to say that his sister, Emily, likes this."

Trap 13. The records are not there

You could be like the great Homer Simpson and simply say, "If at first you don't succeed, give up." Whilst this approach has its attractions, it is not going to take you very far in your search for your ancestors. Often the record is not where you expect it to be. Just because something does not pop up at the click of a mouse button, that doesn't mean that this is the end of the trail.

The TNA website can be of great use to the family historian. It has search tools which can help you determine which records exist and where you can find them. It allows you to search a number of sources, including many local and some private archives. The search results will inform you where those records are located, and whether they are available on-line. However, from experience it can be difficult to navigate through the indexes so it is worth taking the time to try to understand their structure and how they work. The TNA has an on-line research guide which will help you understand them.

If you draw a blank at the TNA, it could be worth contacting the relevant county record office. Archivists are a breed apart and often seem to have innate encyclopaedic knowledge of where and what records are kept. You can also reap dividends from specialist archives. For example, if your ancestor was a miner the National Mining Museum may have something. General searches on the Internet may help - there may be a website dedicated to the area you are looking at, or if you are really lucky, someone may have transcribed and published the record or put the record images on line.

If all else fails, try posting a question on a related forum. There may be someone with knowledge on the area you are looking into. For instance, you might be looking for someone who worked in a specific hospital and the forum could be read by someone who knows exactly what happened to the records when the hospital closed.

Of course, it is inevitable that some records do get lost or destroyed. Parish records which have not yet been transferred to microfilm may have been destroyed in a fire and you might think that the information they held has been lost forever. However, there is always the chance that someone made an earlier transcription. Alternatively, a copy may have been made for the local bishop or archdeacon, or perhaps a local historian or parish council might hold copies.

If you do locate the correct record, but when you search through it the entry you expected is not there, it is worth checking whether there are any gaps in the record. Sometimes pages or periods of time are missing. The reason for this may be written in the record or on accompanying pages, and the explanation might give you an indication of whether the record you are looking for is held elsewhere or was destroyed. You can ask the archivist whether the records from the missing section are held elsewhere or were copied, or whether there is any other document that can give you the information you seek.

"I'm sorry, due to Government cutbacks that series of parish records has been earmarked to run the central heating this week."

Of course, if the records are not there at the moment you want them, it may be that someone else is using them. Be mindful that most people would consider it bad manners to wait until the user has popped off for a break, and then to steal the records for your own use. There's a good chance that they will notice if you substitute a copy of Archive Monthly magazine in its stead.

Trap 14. You don't understand what you have found

So, thought the poor boy called Aladdin, I will just give this tatty old lamp a rub ... and of course, the rest of the story is known - he got the girl, he got the palaces, and the baddy got his comeuppance. He of course didn't know what it was he had found at first.

Sometimes searching brings up something that looks like it might relate to your family, perhaps just a single line of entry, which does not look very interesting at the outset and doesn't seem to make much sense. However, if you discard this record without a second thought, you might be missing out on your own Aladdin's lamp. You may not get a genie but it could help make you a better genealogist.

If the entry you found has your ancestor's name plus some letters or numbers associated with it, this typically could be a transcript produced by someone who has used his/her own letter or number codes as shorthand to cut down on the amount of writing required or data to be captured and stored. To illustrate, you may find a record which has the following written on it:

Smith, Mary (Fras & Ann) 1703 LILLEY HTFD. TR. PR. 343.

At first glance this does not seem show anything meaningful at all. However, you need to establish what this is a record of and where it came from and the first thing to do is look for an explanation of the index.

This example is an on-line record from Pallot's Baptism Index. Reading the associated explanation tells you that this index was originally written on a slip of paper, filed alphabetically, and covered baptisms in the London and surrounding areas generally before the advent of Civil Registration. The entry usually gives the name of the child and parentage, the parish of baptism, and the date of the baptism.

So this can tell us that the name of the child was Mary Smith, her parents were Francis and Ann Smith (Fras being a shortened version of Francis), and that the baptism was conducted in 1703. A quick Internet search will confirm that there is a parish of Lilley in Hertfordshire, which takes care of a further two bits of data. TR and PR are not explained but we can surmise that TR means 'Transcript' and PR means 'Parish Register'. What the number 343 means can only be guessed at but could mean a page number - perhaps in the transcript or the original register. However, decoding this entry might be the clue you were waiting for to tell you that your missing 4 times great-grandfather turned up in Lilley, Hertfordshire.

Pallot was a serial indexer who also recorded early marriages, again up to the onset of Civil Registration. Each slip identifies the church or chapel in which the marriage was celebrated, the names of bride and of groom, whether spinster, bachelor, widow or widower and some-times other details along with the date of the event.

It is not always straightforward to find an explanation if the record has been separated from its original source. You can try looking to see if someone has put an explanation of the terms on line or just google the abbreviation itself to see if anything comes up. If you are in a record office and cannot find an explanation in the book/record/filing index you are researching in – ask the staff, they should be able to help you.

After you have been looking for a while, it is easy just to do searches on random sites and get hits which surprise you. You might, for example, get a reference when looking for your three times great grandmother Fanny Dolittle, which reads like the one below, in a record entitled "Trinity House Petitions" but you might not have a clue what a Trinity House Petition is:

DOLITTLE Fanny, 41, wid of Thomas, of Grimsby, 1849

A quick glance, and at first this is just of a list of people of whom your ancestor is one - nice to see her name in print but there does not seem anything here of particular interest. Finding out what a Trinity House Petition is, however, will give you some good background information on Fanny.

On looking, you would find that Trinity House has been involved with the safety of shipping and the welfare of seafarers since the time of Henry VIII. Petitions to Trinity House were made by merchant sailors or their widows who were seeking financial assistance from the Corporation of Trinity House. They distributed charitable funds entrusted by benefactors for the aid of seafarers and their dependents. So by the fact that Fanny appears on this list, this means she had probably fallen on hard times following the death of her husband, Thomas, who was a seafarer.

But just sometimes, there are abbreviated records that are fiendish to the extreme. One such set of records is the Register of Seamen's Tickets. They can reveal a wealth of detail about the voyages of your seafaring ancestor, but unfortunately the key to understanding the port rotation numbers within them has been lost. Even Alan Turing, the famous Enigma Code breaker, would have found this one a challenge!

Trap 15. You can't travel to get it

There is a Hebrew/Yiddish word - chutzpah - which describes a quality which it is useful to have as a family historian. One modern definition of chutzpah is "gutsy audacity." If you were to find an interesting reference in a book or on-line index, but the actual record is in some distant archive, then a bit of chutzpah might just enable you to see the record in question, without having to travel.

Supposing, through your diligent census searching, you find that one of your ancestors appears to have been in an orphanage. Of course you would like to know more, such as when they arrived there and when did they leave, what happened to their parents and so on. You know that records for that orphanage exist but these are held at a record office some 200 miles away and getting there would be a nightmare. The thing to do is to write to or email the record office in question, preferably not with a demand for information but perhaps with more subtlety.

The following demonstrates how not to make a look-up request: "my granddad was bert james but they always called him lofty except his wife who called him sid but I don't know why. he always had a black dog called snowy which made us laugh. anyhow he was illegitimate and mary always said he'd grown up in an orphanage so would you have anything on him. if it helps he may have had a brother but if he did he died in the first world war because we found a medal and it wasn't berts. he was called snowy because of his mate in the orphanage who had no boots."

So with the above scenario in mind do try to set out what you know as clearly and succinctly as you can. Include vital details such as the census year when they were at the orphanage, their last known address prior to this, plus the date and place of birth. Names of siblings, if you suspect they were at the orphanage, too, could be included. Keep the waffle to a minimum; although you could briefly explain why you are interested in these people, e.g. he is your great-grandfather. State what it is you want to find out about your ancestor. Then ask how much it would cost for a member of their organisation to look your ancestor up in their records and send you an image or a hard copy.

From experience, with this sort of approach, record offices are very obliging and will get back to you very quickly with an estimate of cost.

Generally, charges are very reasonable, and sometimes a kindly archivist will get back to you to say that as the information was very easy to find because of the level and clarity of detail you have given them, they will send you the image/hard copy at no cost whatsoever.

If this does not work, or it is too expensive, there are other options. You could find a family history researcher in the locality of the archive in question and ask them to quote for researching the archives for you. Of course, the more information you can give in advance, the better the results should be. It helps to make a clear distinction between what is from family recollections and what you have found in your researches.

> **Toni's tip:** Try to match with someone living in the area you are interested in who wants research done near to you. You could achieve this through membership of a family history society; in fact some already offer this as a service.

You may also be able to make use of a local family history centre, run by the Church of Jesus Christ of Latter-day Saints (LDS), which are branch facilities of their vast archives of parish records and other resources held in Salt Lake City, Utah. These branches are in a number of places throughout the UK, and might be more convenient to travel to. Sometimes the records you want to look at have to be ordered in advance, so it is best to check first. A small fee is charged for the loan.

Otherwise, there may be an appropriate on-line forum where you can post your query and see if anyone can do a look-up for you. Select your forum carefully as these are often quite specific and may be based on the geographical location, a specific surname or a particular area of research such as military conflicts or army regiments.

> **Kate's comment:** I like to think of a request for help as a finite resource – perhaps as three wishes to be used sparingly and out of necessity. I try to make sure that every request is for something that I could not easily find out for myself. People will quickly recognise if you are being lazy and perhaps won't be so willing to help in the future.

Remember though, whatever approach you make to people, you should consider how much time and effort they will need to make on your behalf. For example if someone offered to walk the dog for you, it would not be appropriate to ask them to pick up a 56lb sack of potatoes on the way back. Likewise if you are asking someone to do a look up at their local record office for you, it would be thoughtless to ask them to photocopy 200 years worth of poor law records for the town of Basingstoke.

Trap 16. You don't know your history

There is an astonishing ignorance amongst the general population about the history that has shaped us. A recent poll of UK towns revealed that the town where people generally know the least in the UK is Swindon, as they were unable to answer questions like "how do you weigh your own head?" The historical knowledge of younger people might also be under threat from the revisionist history which is often to be found in films, particularly those emanating from Hollywood. For example, will the youth of America be aware that the Cuban missile crisis was resolved by the efforts of two international statesmen, John F Kennedy and Nikita Kruschev, and not by a mutant human from the X-men series? Of particular interest must be the potential effect of a film released in 2012, which shows Abraham Lincoln, before he became President, spending his early years as a Vampire hunter. So when it comes to building your historical knowledge, we would suggest you treat the film industry with some degree of caution.

> *Kate's comment:* We do not wish to upset the natives of Swindon, so in the interests of fairness and balance I would like to point out that I was born there, as was my sister and my Dad, and thus Swindon must have produced some knowledgeable people, as we know how to weigh our heads (and without having to remove them first).

The more family history you undertake, the more general history you absorb without even trying. Remarkably rapidly you can become an expert on piano making in Camden in the 19th Century or how Londoners disposed of their sewage before the system built by Bazalgette. It does however pay you to know a few key facts in order to put things into context, and help you understand some of your findings.

Many old documents, such as indentures, refer to the year they were drawn up not by a calendar date but by the number of years into the reign of the current monarch. They are known as regnal years and would be written, for example, 'the 5th year of the reign of George III.'

Toni's tip: *Keep a list of the various monarchs and their reigns handy (mine is helpfully listed on my ruler) – take it with you to record offices and the like for quick look-ups.*

An action that has had repercussions throughout the centuries was the changing of the calendar in 1752 from the Julian system to the Gregorian system. Under the old system, the method of calculating leap years was incorrect and it had been established that the date had got out of step with the seasons. Much of Europe had already adopted the new system so an Act of Parliament in 1750 paved the way for change. Three principal changes occurred: firstly, the formula for calculating leap years changed; secondly, the New Year moved from its previous date of 25th March to the now familiar 1st of January, and thirdly, 11 days were 'dropped' from the calendar. These 11 days were the 3rd to the 13th September 1752 inclusive.

Kate's comment: Even today we can still see the effect of the calendar change. The UK tax year starts on the 6th April. This is because that traditionally annual rents and other fees were payable on the old New Years Day, i.e. 25th March. However, when the change occurred and the 11 days were cut from the calendar, the government adjusted the day so that all rents etc covered a full calendar year. A further 1 day adjustment had to be made to account for a skipped Julian leap year day in 1800. From then onwards the new tax year has started on 6th April.

Before 1752, New Year's Day was the 25th March, so at the time, the dates would go: 24th March 1740, then the next day would be 25th March 1741. When we look back on birth dates and death dates, it can appear, because we are used to the year number changing from end December/beginning of January, as if a baby had died before it was born. To illustrate, you could have someone born on 20th December 1739 and dying on 20th January 1739. They would have been one month old when they died, but when we look at that now, being used to the current system, it appears that the person had died 11 months before they were born. Current reckoning would give a death date of 20th January 1740. Additionally, a person born, say, on the 20th March 1701 and dying on 30th March 1702 would be 10 days old, not one year and 10 days as it looks to us now.

> **Toni's tip:** Get into the habit of writing dates with the full 4 digits for the year. Additionally, for those that fall between the 1st Jan and 25th March which predate the changeover to the new calendar in 1752, record them as 22 February 1712/13. This will bring to your attention that the dates need careful interpretation.

A working knowledge of relevant legislation is useful. Knowing when certain Acts of Parliament were passed is of immense value as often they had a huge influence on social and economic conditions, in many cases directly impacting on your ancestors lives. Examples would be: when were the school acts passed, when did policing begin, what was the impact of the poor laws, and when did the railways come.

Being aware of other key happenings can help explain the migration of your ancestors from their original homes. This would include events such as the Scottish Highland clearances, the impact of religious persecution, and the Irish potato famine.

> **Kate's comment:** My great-great grandfather was born and married in the west of London, near to where the Natural History Museum is now. The census returns for the 1800's show his family moving gradually to the East End. At first I assumed that this was because they were gradually becoming poorer but then I realised these moves were linked to his occupation. He was a leather dealer, and the tanneries of London were moved from the west to the east of London, because they were smelly industries, and if they were located to the east of London, the prevailing winds from the west would take the smell away from most of the population. Many of these unpleasant industries were forced to move in this direction. My relative was simply following the centre of manufacture for the goods he traded in, he was not necessarily suffering financial hardship.

An understanding of the general picture, as well as a feeling for the history of the locality where your ancestors lived, is helpful. This can help explain why, after residing in one place for many years, the family up sticks and move to a city and take up completely different occupations. Something as seemingly innocuous as the repeal of the Corn Laws would have had an immense impact on rural grain-growing areas, and resulted in many people no longer being able to make a living off the land, forcing them into more industrial occupations.

For those that remained in more rural areas, how did they avoid the exodus to the cities and remain in their home villages and towns? Did the railway come to their area? What were the major roads in the area and when did they exist? Were there canals nearby? Did the infra-structure allow for local industries to flourish? Local trade directories are very helpful in giving a contemporary picture of the links between towns such as regular carts and stage routes. Did many of your family die around a particular time and might a smallpox epidemic in the village explain this?

Almost before you know it, you can find you are an expert on historical social conditions, knowledge of old law; historic migration; geographical boundaries and become a desired member of your local pub quiz team!

Trap 17. You didn't check for an index

A recent survey has confirmed what many have long suspected, that some sixty-four percent of men and twenty four percent of women don't read instructions. Of course we accept that real men, along with not eating quiche, do not need to read instructions. However, we suggest that sometimes taking a bit of extra time before wading in may save you lots of time in the long run. So if you are the type of person who doesn't take the time to understand that flange B must fit into groove F first before assembling part K, and manages to make his flat-pack set of bookshelves resemble a coffin, then this section is primarily aimed at you ...

The effectiveness of most on-line indexing can make us a bit complacent, as we grow used to sitting at our computer, filling in the various search fields and then get rewarded with a suitable result. Because of this ease of searching, we can get a bit indignant when we find that the set of records we want to consult is not indexed, be it either an on-line record or book in a record office. The temptation is to launch straight in and start searching page by page. Even with the fastest computer, it is still time-consuming to download image after image to find what we want.

Customarily, we are led to expect indexes to be found at the end of a book, sometimes at the beginning, or sometimes both. Like beauty, indexing does seem to be very much in the eye of the beholder and it is possible to be caught out by the odd individual who has placed his index in the middle of his tome! If you have checked all these places and no index is to be found, look for a separate index. This can take the form of a separate card index or a separate book and it is worth asking the archivist if this is the case if you are working in a record office or archive.

Toni's tip: Of course indexes are fallible, and if you really think that the record should contain an entry for your ancestor, there is no substitute for a real entry-by-entry search. However, make sure you target the search as much as possible to save time. For example if you are trying to pick up a date of entry into a particular institution work backwards from the first time you know they would have had a presence. This can save many a wasted hour.

It is easy to get caught out when using un-indexed records, as Toni's story illustrates:

"I was searching through some workhouse records and, having been caught out before, I had done my normal check to see if there was an index. I checked the front, back and the middle of the book but couldn't find one. So there was nothing to do other than search page by page on several registers. I looked at hundreds of pages that were of no use in order to track down the ones that I needed. Eventually, I investigated another set of related workhouse records, and there I found a separate alphabetical index. This index grouped all the 'A' names together, then the 'B' names and so on, but not in full alphabetical order, e.g. Ascot did not necessarily appear after Abraham. However, it still enabled me to find the date when my ancestor had been admitted or discharged from the workhouse much more quickly and then I could look on the main registers to get the full details."

Of course, if time is not an issue with you, you can take as long as you want to browse through the records. It could be a great way to spend a rainy afternoon. But you have to admit, there are occasions when it is useful to have key information at your fingertips, and can follow a set of instructions. Say if you happened to get a job in bomb disposal and find yourself in a hole that is being shared by an unexploded V2 missile. Whilst undergoing the routine defusing operation, you find an unexpected green wire. What would you do? a) snip it and hope to get off early for a nice cup of tea; b) read through the 2000 page manual to find the relevant action (whilst the timer slowly counts down); or c) look up 'green wire' in the index and act accordingly. Which would you chose to do? If a) or b) is your preference, then perhaps a career in the Civil Service may be more appropriate for you.

Trap 18. My ancestors came from abroad

Foreign ancestry can be a difficult barrier to break down. You may have telltale signs such as an exotic, foreign sounding surname or have been told tales of 'the old country' where your family origins are supposed to be. There may be customs in your family that don't seem to happen in other families, like eating unusual foodstuffs such as reindeer meat at Christmas, when all your friends only have pictures of reindeer on Christmas cards. Or you might be researching your family and be amazed to find that your great-grandfather was born in Germany.

If you have foreign ancestry, there are a number of things it helps to establish. Has your surname been anglicised? Do you have a time frame when your family came to the UK? If you know at least which generation (e.g. great-grandparents) were the immigrants, this will help you target immigration and naturalisation records.

Sometimes a foreign place of birth on a census does not necessarily indicate where the family was rooted, as it could be just a temporary residence abroad. For example, if your ancestor was in the military or foreign service and his wife accompanied him, as often happened, their children may have been born in another country or countries and thus appear to be 'foreign'. If this is the case this can often be confirmed by earlier or later censuses which would show the movement of the family. It should be remembered that it can happen that single men serving abroad in the military or foreign service could marry women from the country they are serving in and this may be the source of your foreign ancestry.

If you can confirm you are definitely from outside of the UK, can you correctly identify the geographical region from within your country of origin? Knowing the name of the area, city or town will help you immensely. Also, can you name at least two generations of the family who were born abroad?

If you can answer most of these questions then you have a good chance of tracking down the family origins. There are on-line passenger and immigration (and emigration) lists that may help; and for many there will be evidence of your adventuring ancestor in the naturalisation records in the TNA. To get further back through the generations though, it will be necessary to search the records of the country concerned.

Like the UK, some countries have on-line access to their records. Using these records may require using subscription sites and there are potential language difficulties if you don't speak the language of your family's country of origin. However, there are some extremely good family history forums in other countries where some contributors may speak English and who may be willing to help you navigate through the records and assist with translation.

Where on-line records do not exist you might have to consider travelling to the country concerned to carry out your researches there. However, a good deal of preparatory work can be done in the UK before travelling, by exploring how the country organises its records. For example, check whether they are held in local, regional or national archives; and how and when they can be accessed. You can look to see if there is a family history society that specialises in ancestry from particular countries or areas, such as the Anglo-German Family History Society. This has the benefit of using local knowledge and expertise in tracing families in the country concerned, including guidance through the records available.

The difficulty comes when all you have to go on is a country of origin and nothing else, but sometimes where a surname is concentrated might help you pinpoint likely origins, if the surname is unusual enough. Using a search engine specific to that country, e.g. ending in .fr for France, or .dk for Denmark and using this in conjunction with on-line translation tools, may provide you with a lead.

If all this sounds too complex and difficult you could consider using the services of a paid local researcher. This has the benefits of their local expertise as well as solves any potential language barriers. It is hard enough trying to understand records in your first language without having to battle through records written in a second, less familiar one.

However, a cautionary note. Supposing your surname is Murphy. You have had several lovely holidays in Ireland, where you have absorbed the culture, drank the Guinness, have an entire set of Riverdance videos, eaten potato-based cuisine, danced to the music and generally felt that you have come home to your roots. You are eager to uncover your origins in the Old Country, so it is a bit unfortunate that when you begin your family history journey, you discover that for several centuries, you have been located in Grimsby and your surname was actually Merfield.

"According to the phrase book this next section is either Registers of Alien Arrivals or UFO sightings in Chinese airspace"

Trap 19. You fail to keep your costs down

When, in 1961, Viv Nicholson won a considerable amount on the Pools, her famous response was that she intended to "spend, spend, spend", which she duly did, on clothes, cars and houses. However, had she been a die-hard genealogist, then the spending would in all likelihood be very different. A big win by a family historian would probably result in subscriptions to all genealogical websites; private research time in archives (as one would no longer wish to associate with the hoi-polloi); a chauffeur-driven limousine to transport you to record offices, and perhaps a nice pair of comfy slippers to stop your feet getting cold. However, if you are not in that lucky position, you will want to keep an eye on your expenditure.

Family history can indeed be an expensive business, and once you have exhausted your family archives, you will need to pay out for things such as certificates, subscriptions or travelling to archives. The opportunities to spend money on family history research are numerous and it can be all too easy to get carried away in the pursuit of 'must haves' when there are free or cheaper alternatives.

As we have already said having a least one family history website subscription is a great advantage. However, if this is not an option, there are many other genealogy sources available that are either free or available for a modest fee. They are often the product of a labour of love by volunteers who diligently transcribe records and can give you access to transcriptions of birth, marriage and death indexes; census and parish registers.   These may be web-based or they may only available by sending off for them in a CD or booklet form or find them at family history fairs, or sometimes they may only be available over the web, either free or for a fee. There is also growing accessibility to images of original documents, such as parish registers that are being made available for free. However, it should be noted that for all these resources the coverage is patchy. Additionally, there is no consistency of details transcribed and you have to search for them, as they are spread all over the place.

Kate's comment: The rate of progress for records to be included on volunteer sites depends on how many volunteers are available to carry out the work. If the records you want are not yet available there is always a chance they will be at a later date. If you have time on your hands, perhaps you could offer your help!

Using these free resources alone is unlikely to give you a full picture of your family history. One of the key elements of doing this is to use census returns, but to gain comprehensive access to these you will either have to subscribe to an on-line provider or travel to a place which holds them, such as a record office, archive or family history centre. This is fine if you happen to live within walking distance of one of these, but for most of us this will involve time and expense to get there.

> **Toni's tip:** Look to see whether your local library offers free access to any major commercial family history websites. An occasional bus ride to the library would be much cheaper than a costly annual subscription, if your demand for that site is quite modest. It may be also be useful if you already have access to UK-based records, but your library offers wider scope, e.g. a world-wide subscription.

So it is best to be selective over what you are going to spend your hard-earned cash on and take into consideration things like:

- How much time do you have to spend on this hobby? Can you get the information you need from a source near to you, rather than incurring the cost of travel to a major archive? Can a county record office or family history centre supply you with the information you need rather than travelling to a national archive?
- How long will it take you to travel to an archive? Will you have sufficient time to research thoroughly when you get there, or will you have to travel there on more than one occasion? If you do need to visit on more than one occasion, would it be more cost-effective to stay overnight nearby rather than make two trips?

Your local library can be a very valuable tool for your research. Libraries often have free access to various resources such as national and local newspaper archives. You might also find that your library will hold copies of other types of records, such as census, parish or civil registration indexes. Some even offer remote on-line access to archive material if you are a member. It is always worth contacting them to find out what they have.

Many commercial sites will allow you to use their search facilities for free but will restrict how much of the results you can see. They do this of course to tempt you into paying your money to see the full Monty. In some cases, with a little effort and lateral thinking, you may be able to save money and use these partial results to get what you want. For example, it is possible to get the names of most or all family members from a census, without actually seeing the census entry itself. This can allow you to make sense of family groups and eliminate wrong candidates before you pay out for subscriptions or viewings. So, if time is available to you, sit down and have a play around.

Websites generally offer a pay-per-view option, so if you do not need to look at many entries, this could work out a lot cheaper for you. However, this option does not allow you to browse so you have to ensure you have the correct entry before you pay to look at it; there are no refunds for selecting the wrong record to view.

An interesting development is the increasing use of collaborative projects using volunteers to transcribe documents, such as those being undertaken by organisations like Family Search and the TNA. Typically, un-indexed images are initially made available on-line, then volunteers transcribe them. These transcriptions are then linked to the image so that these documents become fully searchable. Even some commercial companies are involving volunteers in transcribing records.

A growing number of specialist archives and record offices are offering on-line access to their collections in the form of time-limited passes. Depending on the organisation, for a fairly low cost you may be able to have, say, a 24-hour, one week, one month or three month pass. Using these could be good value for money as they avoid the need for travel or certificate purchase.

Here again, forums can be useful, but don't expect others to do your entire family history for you. Be prepared to share information you have found with your correspondents as well, it should work both ways.

And one further thought. If you follow our suggestions you may have saved yourself a bit of money and can now buy a second copy of this book to give to your friend (as a family historian, you probably don't have more than one).

Trap 20. You overlook other sources of help

There are some poor, sad souls out there to whom genealogy means very little. They tend to equate the art of family history research with other pastimes such as trainspotting or making scrapbooks of 'Pylons I Saw On My Holiday', and really they don't understand what a richly rewarding and fascinating hobby it is. Like these other ways of spending your time, finding out about your family can be a fairly isolated activity. Genealogists generally do not hunt in packs.

But there are an awful lot of us. Some may band together and form a county family history society or attend regular U3A (University of the Third Age) meetings, but generally we are all diligently working in our homes on our own and not necessarily aware of all those others involved in the same activity as us. Which is a shame, as the collective knowledge held by all those brains would be a powerful tool.

Collaboration with others can be very rewarding and enjoyable. Two brains are most definitely better than one. Dialogue with someone else who is researching the same family can result in each of you finding that the other holds the key to unlocking a puzzle that has frustrated you. Simply discussing a brick wall situation with another like-minded person can bring up suggestions such as: 'have you tried this site', or 'did you know about this organisation' or even, if they are involved in the same family as you: 'Oh, I know the answer to that mystery, she was his second wife...'

There are plenty of specialist magazines and family history society journals where people will publish their surname interests or even requests for help on something more specific. Many magazines actively encourage their readership to write in with problems and may have a panel of experts who will attempt to answer your questions. Some also throw such queries open to the rest of their readership to see if anyone else can solve the problem. Joining a local family history society and attending their meetings can throw you into the path of more experienced family historians who may be generous with their time and help you break down that brick wall.

Some of the best sources of help can be found on-line. Have a look to see if there is a parish website for the village your ancestors came from. Whilst many of these just concentrate on present day happenings and council business, we have found many others that have a slant towards local history and contain historical documents such as discussions on village 'elders' and other village characters, old village trades and businesses; and sometimes a forum where people can post their interests. Kate has experienced this: "I was able to establish that the family I was researching had not originated from the town of Saffron

Walden, Essex, but had moved in and out of the town within a few decades. I discovered that because the Parish Council had published a pre-1841 village census on their website, and the family was not on it!"

As said previously in trap 15, forums are often organised by specialism. The majority of forums require you to register your details but once registered with them you can post details of your request for information. The generosity of people on these forums can be amazing; we have known individuals who have gone to local record offices to look up information for someone whom they only know through contact on a forum.

Toni has direct experience of this: "On one occasion I posted a message on a Birmingham-based forum asking whether anyone had access to records for a particular church. I had an ancestor that I knew had moved about 150 miles south from Birmingham, but I did not know specifically where he came from or when he made the move. I had identified a potential marriage for him back in Birmingham from a transcript, but needed the full entry to establish whether he was my man. Within 15 minutes someone had posted a reply which gave me the answer I sought. Other postings have resulted in pictures of specific old pubs I have been seeking information on, or newspaper articles that I sought."

Kate's comment: It will be appreciated if you stick to the area in which the forum is set up to cover. There is little point in posting your own personal insights into NHS reforms if the site is about workhouse infirmaries.

Don't worry about being a forum 'newbie'. If you don't know how to go about asking for information - admit it! We have found that people are very kind and will willingly guide you through the process. The chances are, that whatever your query, albeit a question about a distant relative, or what happened to the records from a particular parish church, there will be someone who can answer you. You will be hard pushed to find a topic so obscure that there isn't someone who could use it as their specialist subject were they to appear on "Mastermind". We are willing to bet that there is someone who knows all the colloquial or dialect words for 'turnip' ever used in the United Kingdom - and if it is you, it isn't necessary to let us know, as our interest is strictly limited.

"In Upper Beachingham before the reformation turnips were known as 'The Kings Knobblers', but after this ....drone........drone.........drone....."

Raiders of the lost archives

Visiting and Using Archives and Record Offices

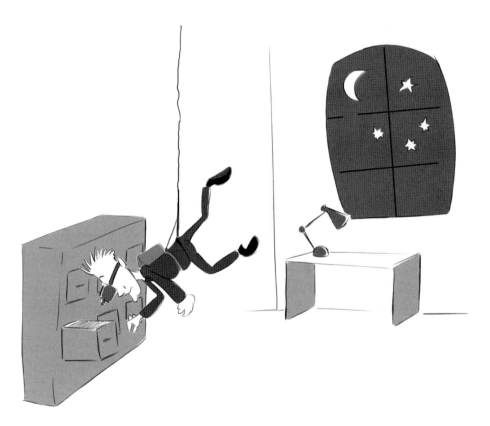

"If only Arthur had realised that there was free public access to the records, it would have saved him a lot of bother"

Trap 21. You did insufficient planning

There is a spectrum of spontaneity. At one end lie people whose individual tasks are approached with military precision, to those at the other end who teeter headlong from one activity to another, without giving any thought to what they are doing. Most of us employ some kind of planning, such as writing a shopping list when going to the supermarket, or compiling a 'to do' list when preparing for a holiday. People who do little, or no, planning for an activity may be very spontaneous but they run the risk of whatever they are doing turning into an absolute disaster and waste of time, simply because something important has not been considered in the first place.

There are occasions when thinking things through fully in advance of taking action, is fairly essential. A classic example of this took place after WW1. The French decided they wanted to build a strategic defence against invasions from the east (in other words, from Germany again). This was promoted by the then French Minister of War, André Maginot, and in his honour the line of defence was named after him. The Maginot Line, a series of concrete fortifications, tank obstacles, machine-gun posts and so on was constructed along France's borders with Germany. It was a pity, then, that the French did not extend the line along the border shared with Belgium. This left a country-wide gap which enabled the German army to sweep round, completely avoiding the need to attack the line and allowing France to be conquered in a matter of days. The Maginot Line was costly to build, expensive to maintain and ultimately useless, simply because the French had not planned for an attack via Belgium.

Whilst in all likelihood you will never have to plan a defence against a hostile country, you might need to consider planning for the next stage of your family history research, which could involve a trip to an archive. You can, of course, just decide to make a visit on a whim, and whilst the visit may be enjoyable and you might turn up something interesting about your family, it may not be the best use of your time. You will get much more out of the visit if you decide in advance what you would like to focus on and achieve during your visit.

It helps to know in advance what records are in the archive you are visiting. Many record offices and archives have on-line catalogues that can be searched. For example, the TNA website has links to several different catalogues relating to their holdings and those of other record offices. Sometimes these can be difficult to navigate, but with a bit of perseverance it is possible to identify the exact book, document or record series you want. After you have identified the records you wish to consult, just check whether they are available on-line. Sometimes it is worth paying a small fee to download a document rather than go to the expense of travelling to the archive to look at it.

Also don't assume that just because your ancestors came from a particular place that all the records relating to that ancestor will be found in the relevant county archive. For example, there may be some information about a Brighton railway worker in the East Sussex Record Office, but if you wanted to know about his employment, the records are probably in the TNA, where many railway staff records are kept. So if you do your homework first, you won't have a wasted journey.

Toni's tip: I try to concentrate on just a couple of individuals at a time in my tree. I think about their lives, and what evidence they may have left behind them. Then I see whether records relating to these events for the right period are held in any archive. For example, if you were lucky enough to have an ancestor who worked as a 19th century palaeontologist, you might be able to locate his staff diary at the Natural History Museum archives.

It is a good idea to prepare a list of the records you wish to search. This list should incorporate details such as the title of each record; its reference number; and what form it takes, such as microfilm, microfiche, document, book, computer record and so on. This will tell you whether you will need to book in advance a microfilm or fiche reader, a computer, a desk or map table. Bookings can often be made by email and that means you can organise your day, say, by booking a microfiche reader in the morning and a computer in the afternoon.

If there is no on-line catalogue or you cannot work out from the one available what it is you need, then email or telephone the office to clarify. The staff who work at archives are generally very helpful and will guide you through the procedure. It is particularly important to contact the record office beforehand if it is one which holds records at more than one site, as you may have to order what you want in advance so that they can get it to the site you are visiting. Assistance can usually be found through the record office's website. It can give you a lot of useful information, such as what items you can take into the archives with you, such as laptops and cameras; and any restrictions placed on their use e.g. no flash photography.

> **Toni's tip:** *There is usually a limit to how many records you can order in advance, e.g. a maximum of 4 documents. Ordering documents in advance can really speed up your day, as they will be there ready and waiting for you, and makes sure you use every precious moment of research time.*

In general you will need (although it will vary according to the office):
- A desk to look at original documents such as electoral registers, workhouse records, deeds, manorial records, school records etc, which you may need to book
- A map table to look at Ordnance Survey maps, enclosure maps, tithe maps, or estate maps.
- A computer to access digital images and the Internet for family history or local history research purposes – some offices have subscriptions to commercial websites which can help supplement or confirm your findings there and then.
- A microfilm/or microfiche reader to look at parish registers, censuses and newspapers, for images still held in this medium.

However, don't be tempted to book everything for the whole day as this is unfair to other users and will annoy the archivists. It does pay to let the office know of any special needs you may have, such as extra room around a table for wheelchair access.

And lastly, before you set out, or reserve your train seat or book your B&B, just check that the archive is open for your intended day of visit. After all, you wouldn't want all your diligent, military-style planning to fall down, simply because the archive employees have gone on their annual booze cruise to Ostend.

Trap 22. You are ill-equipped for the day

Do you ever suffer from anxiety dreams? If you are a very organised person yet you worry that you have not prepared properly for your record office visit, just imagine the anxiety dreams that you could experience. *You are sitting naked in the reading room, desperately trying to cover your shame with a copy of Burke's Peerage (which isn't big enough); your pencils are all blunt; your notebooks have decided to float away on the breeze, and the archivist is angrily demanding you produce identification (which is a bit difficult as you have no clothes and therefore no pockets to keep it in).* When you wake up, in a cold sweat, you will probably decide to turn to stamp collecting, instead, it is much safer and you need never to go out of your house again.

So if you want to stop the worrisome dreams, get prepared before-hand. Start with the practical details, like making sure you know where you are going, what the opening times are, whether there is easily accessible long term parking nearby and what it will cost; or how you can get there by public transport. Check whether refreshments are available on site or nearby - you might want to take a packed lunch.

Take the things you need with you:

- The information you have prepared such as dates, places, names and family tree
- The list of records you want to consult, with details of any earlier searching you may have carried out
- Your reader ticket, which is needed to access original documents in most archives. Many local authority record offices use the County Archives Research Network system (CARN). You can sign up for this at any participating office and use the same reader ticket at all archives utilising this system. Other archives have their own systems and some may need a photo in order for a reader's ticket to be issued. In each case you will need to check with the record office to see what form of identification they require
- Pencils and pencil sharpener (pens are not usually permitted)
- Notebook or scrap paper to make notes on
- Digital camera – this is a wonderful way of recording documents and can give excellent results. Make sure it is fully charged and/or take spare batteries. Check first that the record office allows them
- Take your laptop and ensure it is fully charged in case you do not have access to mains power. Again, make sure you check that the record office allows its use

- Money, including change:
  - ~ for photocopying or copies of images
  - ~ if you wish to purchase copies of records made by the office. You may be able to pay by cash or cheque but credit or debit cards may not be accepted
  - ~ for the drinks/snacks machine
  - ~ as you may be asked to pay for a photography licence; you may be able to purchase a daily, weekly, monthly or yearly permit.

> *Kate's comment:* Make sure you are wearing comfortable clothing for the day, it can be a hot summer's day outside the record office, but feel cold inside in the temperature-controlled environment that is necessary for the preservation of records.

And if you forget to take your reading glasses, don't be surprised if you have to visit the archive a second time. You might have spent two hours searching the Guild of Farriers records, only to later find those were the Guild of Curriers instead.

Trap 23. You underestimate the task in hand

Your authors have a wide range of abilities and skills between them - for example, Toni in particular is highly organised and structured in her day to day task management, and Kate is late for everything. Toni has attempted (on numerous occasions) to persuade Kate that the reason for her total lack of punctuality is down to the fact that she is unable to allow sufficient time for each of the tasks she has to perform, e.g., Toni gets a 'phone call from Kate stating that she just has to: "brush hair, put on make-up, walk the dog, feed the chickens, answer some emails, do the week's shopping and therefore will be 'round in about 40 minutes." This lack of appreciation of the time tasks take to perform leads to her running over the amount of time she has mentally put aside to get the whole of these tasks completed and therefore she ends up leaving her house late. Kate, it must be said, nods in agreement when Toni stresses this, but acknowledges quietly to herself that the reason she is always late is really because she cannot be arsed to get out of bed on time.

Realistically, however, the majority of us are very poor at estimating how long a particular task will take and it is very easy to fall into the trap of believing a single visit to a record office will be sufficient to gain all the knowledge needed to complete our family researches. Those who have already become used to doing research on line, especially with records that have been conveniently indexed for us, become accustomed to spending just a few minutes on each individual search. It is, of course, very different when you do not have an index and you have to perform a manual search, item by item, actually turning real pages or moving the microfilm from one frame to the next.

Before embarking on your searches you might, for instance, set aside an hour to look for your grandfather's railway employment record. Three and a half hours later you find it. It took so long, because the records have been organised by employee start date, and not in alphabetical order. Ironic, really, as you were trying to find his employee records so you could find out when he started work there!

Carrying out manual searches may not seem to hold much in the way of advantage compared to the modern digital methods of research, but you do get a better 'feel' for the time period and people you are looking at. You may start to recognise family names, local trades, the relative wealth of the area or even factors that were killing people off. Some of the names which crop up regularly could belong to people who were known to your ancestors - perhaps friends, or wider family, or even business acquaintances.

> ***Kate's comment:*** *When in a record office looking for baptism records for one of my family lines, one surname kept appearing in the microfilm records. It was an unusual name, Gerrish, and in sufficient numbers that they became very noticeable - a case of, 'Oh no, not <u>another</u> one!' However, at a later time, I found a marriage record which showed that my great great grandmother had been Amelia Gerrish before marriage - and so those baptism records I had noticed were in the main for distant relatives of mine. So I knew straight away that Amelia had come from a family which was large and well established in the town where they lived.*

It's worth taking a note of anything that looks like it is connected to your family, such as details of a surname which is vaguely similar to the one you are looking for. You may be trying to track a specific person but do not dismiss someone in the right area with the same or similar surname - this could be a relative and could help point you towards the person you are trying to track, and to build your family tree. Analysis of this information at a later date may enable you to fit these people into your family history or to eliminate them completely. This is a much more efficient use of your time rather than trying to analyse it all whilst at the record office.

Anyone new to archive searching will probably underestimate the time that tasks will take. They will need to manage their expectations of what can be achieved in the time available. Accept that you will not be able to get through everything on your list and that another visit will probably be necessary at a later date.

Having said that, it is still a useful thing to take a generous list of what records you would like to search, because as visits to record offices for most of us involve a fair amount of travel, you do not want to waste this by having insufficient to do once there. You might need to abandon a search if it is not proving successful. Having other options for search areas is useful. It might be that you just need a change to a different type of format, say from microfilm to paper-based, as concentrating for a long time on one record format can be very tiring, and when you are tired you fail to spot things or make mistakes.

By the time you have read for the third time that Selina Petty has had an illegitimate son, Percy, baptised on 28th November 1798, you know you should stop and have a break. This is where you need to note what record you are searching and where you started and finished. Clear recording of what you have already looked at will stop you going through the same records later and reading about Selina and son for yet another time.

Toni's tip: *If you didn't record your findings directly into your laptop, make sure you write up your notes as soon as possible. It is surprising how quickly you can forget the clever system of abbreviations you constructed on the day and can end up with pages of unusable detail.*

It does also make sense to establish the opening hours of the archive you are visiting as you don't want to be half-way through a promising set of records only to have to leave because the office is about to close. When you see the archivists with their coats on and jangling their keys, you know you are outstaying your welcome, and rest assured, they take a dim view of any attempts to 'borrow' records even if you do promise to bring them back the next day.

"Is that a Vivienne Westwood designer outfit do you think?

Trap 24. You fall foul of the rules

Being an ardent family historian with sufficient obsessive drive to visit remote and uninviting archives is usually something found only in one, often slightly odd, member of the family (yes, that's you). If you do manage to persuade your significant other that they want a trip to Cheshire, they will probably be more willing to drop you off at the record office and go on to visit the fleshpots of Chester rather than have a day with you in a shady, air-conditioned record office. So if you do have a friend or family member to share your outing, this can be very pleasant. Toni derives great pleasure from having days out at a record office with her father as they both enjoy sharing their breakthroughs with each other and two can of course achieve much more in a day than can one person. However, the family hereditary trait towards deafness can pose a difficulty:

"A typical conversation with my father on arrival at a county record office goes along the lines of me saying softly: 'Dad we need to sign in here' and Dad saying (in booming voice) **'Do we need to sign in somewhere?'**. I will then face him directly and say, in softer voice, 'Yes, we sign-in at the desk here, they will need to see your Readers ticket' and Dad replying **'Do I need my ticket thingy?"** and so it goes on. I do try to get him to modulate his voice to a whisper, but he still manages a whisper at around 90 decibels!"

"Worse still is when we are in the actual search rooms. I try to have everything prepared and give him a typed list of records to search and search criteria. I also fill in the forms and request the appropriate records for him. But inevitably a short conversation will be necessary to get him underway, and it is unfortunate that the entire search room with be privy to this conversation. I don't want us to fall foul of the rules of the search room, and I really appreciate that conversation in the room should be kept to a minimum and at a whisper, but it can just be so difficult to comply sometimes."

" 'Ere, Toni, these WW1 records show that Great Uncle Bill had the clap!"

We don't want to put you off the idea of visiting record offices so we have here a few hints as to how to make your day stress-free and fun. We know this stuff is a bit dull so we gave you these tedious acronyms. You may wish to memorise these. Or on the other hand, you may prefer to have a life.

1. When handling documents, have some **R.E.S.P.E.C.T.**

✝ **R**est your open book on the stands provided. These are often foam wedges and using these minimises the strain on the spine of the book and keeps it in good condition.

✝ **E**nsure loose leaf items are put back in order.

✝ **S**aliva on a page often offends and also damages old records, so don't lick your fingers before turning a page. You might be asked to wear gloves if you are using very precious records.

✝ **P**encils are best used to make notes and in most cases pens are not allowed in the search rooms as ink can cause permanent damage to fragile and irreplaceable documents.

✝ **E**visceration of pages is strictly forbidden (ok highfaluting word used as nothing else fitted but what we mean is don't cut out chunks from a document).

✝ **C**are is needed when turning pages of old documents to avoid tearing them.

✝ **T**aking notes should be done with the paper to the side of the documents, not on top, otherwise you could cause indentations.

2. Comply with security arrangements, don't be a **G.I.T.**

✝ **G**ood researchers work out a list of what they need in advance so that they don't take large bulky folders into the search rooms – which are often not allowed in anyway because of the possibility of theft of records.

✝ **I**nner wear only – outerwear, (i.e. coats) should be left in the lockers provided along with any bags you might have brought with you.

✝ **T**ransparent pencil cases are useful so that security can easily see what you are taking into the search rooms with you.

3. Don't be a pain in the **N.E.C.K.**

✝ **N**icking another person's microfilm viewer or table is disrespectful

✝ **E**ncroaching papers from another researcher into your personal workspace is annoying.

✝ **C**onversations should be kept to a minimum and always done as quietly as possible.

✝ **K**eep mobile phones in the lockers or turn them to vibrate only – and don't use them in areas where people are working!

> **Toni's tip:** If, like me, you happen to be allergic to dust, you might like to take some antihistamines before a visit to a record office, as dust could be described as a hazard of the job. It's probably best to take the non-drowsy tablets as not only does loud and persistent sneezing annoy archivists, but they have also been known to get irritated with loud and persistent snoring.

Trap 25. The staff weren't helpful

You may imagine your average archivist as being someone who is old, dry, bookish and possessive with the documents in their care – a bit like a librarian but with added dust – but the reality is usually quite different. The aim of most archivists is to help you, the researcher, to find your way around the records and to advise you on how to use the equipment and catalogues and they are knowledgeable and welcoming. They are interested in their job and understand what you are trying to achieve, but they are also likely to be busy and have many pressures on their time.

The Archivist's Tale

An imaginary, but typical, day in the life of an average archivist

Sarah is an archivist. She arrives at work at 8.55 and is settled at her desk by 9.00. She starts her computer and opens the first of her 37 email queries. This is from a lady writing a history of pies, who wants to know what records are available on this subject. Sarah writes a nice reply with a few suggestions for search areas. Emails two and three are straightforward queries about opening hours, which she responds to, with a polite suggestion that they look at the website for any potential changes to opening hours.

The first wave of researchers has now arrived, and Sarah processes requests for document retrieval from storage. She discovers that a register of non-conformist church records appears to have had its pages stuck together by chewing gum and forwards this for repair. She returns to her unopened emails that now number 43. After arranging a date to give a family history society a guided tour she explains to another corres-

pondent that no, he can't bring his pet rat with him into the records office, no matter how well behaved she is.

Directing her assistant to help the old gentleman re-wind the microfiche rolls that have somehow gone awry, she organises the delivery and cataloguing of a new set of local militia records. Unable to ignore the dull ache in her bladder and the increasingly noisy rumbles in her stomach, she goes to lunch, stopping en-route to explain to a newbie researcher that she can't take records home as this isn't a lending library, it is an archive.

After a brief lunch and loo break, she is in to a meeting to discuss the next stage of the digitisation process to increase remote accessibility to records. She manages to complete half of a grant application towards the cost of a student placement to help with the digitisation process before breaking off to deal with an irate member of the public who wants to know why he can't have one to one help with his family tree. She snatches a quick cup of coffee before answering a letter from a lady who has offered the archive her late father's photograph collection of local village events.

She then spends some quiet time returning the records to their storage area in the basement before being called to investigate reports of a rat running round the reading room. She locks up at 5.30, taking home an outline of a leaflet she is working on to help people understand how to use poor law records – she hopes to get this finalised this evening after she has cooked dinner for her family.

So if you approach an archivist and tell them that your name is Brown and your family came from the area, and you want to know what information is held about them, then you are not likely to get a very helpful reply. This is not because the archivist is unhelpful, but that they are not there to actually do your research for you. And no matter how fascinating and exciting are the things you discover, it is unlikely that the archivist will have sufficient time to listen to you recounting the wondrous facts about your 3 x great grandfather's seafaring exploits. Instead, he/she may well be thinking about the huge list of things that needs to be done that day.

Try to see it from their point of view. They have a hard job – and often these services are the first to experience cutbacks in funding, and this may mean that their employees are even more stretched and stressed by being short-staffed. Also, some archives can have 10 miles or more of shelving over several floors, so to expect an archivist to know what and where everything is and how much of it relates to your family is a bit unrealistic!

26. You can't find what you are looking for

It is fact of life that items are not always where they are supposed to be. Car keys, important notes, biros, mobile phones and reading glasses apparently have an innate ability to move when your back has turned – in the case of reading glasses, often to reappear by stealth on the top of the user's head when least expecting it and after a 20 minute fruitless search. Items will also take it upon themselves to swap locations so when you find your pen in the refrigerator it's a fair bet that it has exchanged places with the Wensleydale currently occupying your handbag. Quantum physics no doubt allows for such items to exist simultaneously in fridge and handbag but really what has happened is that you are so busy with your mind on very important things that you have accidentally put the pen/Wensleydale/car keys etc in the wrong place without noticing.

It is unsurprising therefore that with such a lot of records, items will be missing or mis-located in a busy records office. We are all human and prone to putting things into the wrong place, and even in the most secure records offices, some things do get pilfered. When, therefore, you have looked for a specific record or entry and you don't find it, have another look just in case you missed it first time round. It is easy to have a lapse of concentration when you are looking at a large number of records and your eyes could have skated right past what you are searching for. If you still don't find it, check that all the records are there, such as numbered microfiche sheets, or if loose-leaf records are being used, check that they are in sequence. If after this, check with the archivist because it is possible that the document may have been removed for preservation or simply lost and they may have infor-mation to this effect.

If the records are complete yet you still can't find what you are looking for – reconsider why you think that record should be there. Have you got everything right so far? Could it be that the family were in a different place at that time? Think a little out of the box, for example, if a baptism is involved, and it was the first child, could he/she be baptised in the mother's maiden name because she wasn't yet married, or baptised in the mother's parish of birth?

When Archivists Turn Bad .....

Records of course do get lost or destroyed and it is possible that a gap exists for the period you are interested in, and there maybe nothing you can do to find the information you want. Sometimes the documents are available but in such poor condition that they cannot be used. Perhaps ask the archivist to see if there are any other relevant records which cover the time period you are interested in. By way of illustration, if you are looking for a record of entry to a workhouse in about 1879 but the admission records are not available, it may be that you might find information in the workhouse Religious Creed Registers for the same time period. Whilst this might not give you everything you want to find, they can give some interesting information such as the date of admission and discharge, as well as the religious denomination.

Toni's tip: *I wanted to consult a settlement examination for Elizabeth Nebbard in an archive I was visiting some years ago. I had the reference, but the document could not be located. There is every possibility that it had simply been mis-filed and would turn up some day but it was frustrating at the time to not be able to put my hands on it. One day I will go back and see if it has turned up! For this hobby you need a good system of notes and a very good memory, and not be in a rush to get your family history finished.*

Trap 27. I didn't want to look like a newbie

The comic potential of a newcomer to an activity who pretends to know what to do and then makes a complete fool of himself is something that has been well used by sketch writers. Someone trying not to show themselves to be utterly ignorant – and failing – is worth a good snigger to those of us in the know. Kate once had the delight of having ultrasound treatment to a wound which was not healing properly. On the first occasion, the operator said that she might 'feel a small tingling' which Kate assured her she could. The operator, deliberately straight-faced, let her know that the machine hadn't at that point been switched on ..... and at the next appointment, Kate kept quiet.

A record office can seem a bit of a challenge for the uninitiated, as all the researchers there seem to know what they are doing and are whizzing through filing cabinets and setting up microfiche machines in a quiet bustle of efficiency. You could waste a lot of time and effort trying to work out how everything should be done, and none of us like to look stupid. So if you are new to the system, be honest with the archivist/receptionist and explain that this is your first visit to a record office, say what you want to look at that day, and ask if there is anything they can tell you to help get you started. Before you can say

'The Apprenticeship Records of the Worshipful Company of Girdlers 1449 – 1683' the art and mysteries of the archive retrieval system could be revealed to you in all its glory.

> **Toni's tip:** *It may feel like you are wasting time, but if the office offers a tour think seriously about taking it – it will almost certainly mean you will be more efficient in your research, knowing exactly where you should be looking. At the same time it may make you aware of groups of records that will be helpful to you.*

Most record offices share a similar system for their microfilm and microfiche parish records. It has been designed to be as straight-forward and self-explanatory as possible, as well as providing a method whereby everyone knows when a record has been taken out for perusal, and who has taken it out. Typically, it works thus:

Once you have secured your microfilm or microfiche reader, you will see that there is a numbered empty microfilm box or numbered microfiche card associated with the number of the machine you are using. You will need to hold on to this for the next stage of your record retrieval. You then need to look on top of the parish record microfilm/ microfiche cabinets where some loose-leaf books are stacked. These books contain a list of all the parish records, held in alphabetical order. There is usually a separate page for each parish, with a breakdown of what records are held, the time periods they are held for, and what form they are available in, such as microfilm, microfiche or original. There will be a reference number relating to each record, and you can make a note of the reference number you require and then look in the filing cabinets to find the record matching this reference number. You then swap this record with your empty microfilm box or microfiche card. This enables you to return the record once you have finished with it to the correct location, and also allows other users to identify who has that particular record, should it be required by them.

> **Kate's comment:** *All hobbies and interests have equipment and language associated with them and family history is no different. Abbreviations and acronyms are used and if you come up against something you are not sure of, then look around, as there are often guides to the text used in that particular office.*

Theoretically, once you have mastered the techniques of using a microfilm machine, then you should be able to operate all microfilm machines as they are generally the same in all record offices – but naturally, this is not so. Toni says: "Whether it is my left-handedness or that I am manually challenged, I have a complete lack of affinity with machines such as microfilm readers, and I have never truly grasped the knack of using them. Usually each microfilm reader has a helpful laminated card stuck to it, with a clear diagram showing exactly how the film should be threaded into the machine. It looks perfectly straightforward at first but soon manages to go completely haywire. I have been known to fail even before I try to load the film into the machine, by simply attempting to take off the protective wrapper the film comes with, only to drop the whole lot on the floor and watch it unravel as it travels across the room."

"Move along please, nothing to see, all under control"

"Sometimes after feeling all pleased with myself after having successfully negotiated the 'threading up' of the machine I then proceed to wind the film on. At this point it is recommended that you stop and think. For inevitably I will then wind the wrong way, immediately unthreading the thing again. Worse still is where you have a motorised winder. It takes time to get a feel for the speed of the motor, and I can be a little too heavy on the pressure I apply, and the result is about two miles of film unspooling all over the place. Of course, I try to act calm and nonchalant as if I meant to do that all along – a bit like a cat that falls off the back of the sofa whilst asleep."

Of course, with a little practice most normal people can grasp the procedures reasonably efficiently but if you are struggling, ask the staff to help. With luck and a fair wind, however, all this may be a thing of the past as more archives ditch the microfilm in favour of the digital image – something that cannot happen too soon for Toni and the record offices she visits.

Trap 28. I think I already looked at that

The Internet, radio, television and newspapers are full of information regarding health issues. When you log in/switch on/open up your media of choice, you will sooner or later come across someone offering you help and advice about the symptoms you weren't even aware you had, and eventually you will discover you have a 'syndrome'. It seems almost daily that a new syndrome comes into being and we feel strongly that we should be joining this information wave. So this is your introduction to 'Genealogists Déjà vu Syndrome' or GDS for short.

The symptoms for this debilitating and chronic condition are feelings of irritation, frustration and glumness, as you have an overwhelming sense of having looked at something before, at least once if not twice.

Although this sounds a worrying condition, fear not, there are things you can do to prevent its onset. The most important thing is to realise what the cause of this syndrome is, namely the process of looking at the same record for a second or subsequent occasion. If a record was not particularly helpful or interesting in the first place, it will be even less so if you look at it more than once and will also be a waste of your valuable time.

Kate's comment: We know of someone (who will remain anonymous) who has not only purchased a wrong death certificate, but has bought it twice, because he had not checked his records!

The way to prevent you researching the same record set twice is to make a note of what you have searched, and make sure that you keep that note attached to the relevant family history. If in the future you revisit this history to see what else you can do with it – and historians do a lot of that – you will know what you had done first time around and will not be repeating the same thing. It is easy to be irritated by, for example, your inability to find a specific part of your family history, such as just precisely where and when your three times great grandparents Annie and William were married. You might decide to revisit this problem, and spend a long time analysing the records from likely places they may have married, based on evidence such as where their first child was born or where families of their surname were known to live. Chances are that you would be following precisely the same route as you had done the first time around and not surprisingly fail again to find what you are looking for – because it is not there. However, if you had made clear notes about what you had already done for this history, you would know not to do the same things again but to vary your pattern of searching.

Toni's tip: Keep a dedicated running note in the back of your working file of all the records you have already researched, including the record office reference, the dates covered, when searched and the results of that search. Check this list before planning your next record office visit and determining what records you will need to inspect this time around.

For those who prefer to rely on memory alone, bear in mind that we tend to store the more bizarre facts we come across, but not retain things that are uneventful or uninteresting. This is not always useful with family history. So when we set out to search, for example, the parish burials for Little Snoreham 1783 – 1807, we probably wouldn't remember that we had already done so two years previously. That is, until our memory is triggered by reading a comment made by the church incumbent, at the end of the register, which said the old parish gravedigger, Septimus Runt, had 'fallen into a new-dug grave as a result of his indulgence in cheap gin.' Whilst it gives you a chance to appreciate this entertaining revelation for a second time, it also brings it home that you have spent the last three hours duplicating a fruitless search.

Trap 29. You waste time

The American writer Ambrose Bierce defined a day as: "A period of twenty-four hours, mostly misspent." If you are going to make the effort to travel to a record office, you do not want to misspend the time there by experiencing distractions that are going to take you away from the serious work of researching your family history. However, distractions exist aplenty and we will deal with the two main ones here.

1. The self-inflicted distraction. Of course, record offices are full of dry, dusty tomes that are really of interest only to the truly dedicated. However, with them may be found nuggets of fascinating facts that can draw in the unwary person. You might find that a catalogue of garden implements from the 17th century is incredibly interesting and before you know it, you have spent an hour on the dibber makers of East Anglia rather than looking for the will of your great great grandfather. Equally, an interesting or unusual name can leap out at you and before you know it you have been logging all incidences of the 'Dickhuph' family in Aberystwyth instead of chasing your Welsh mining ancestry. One of the joys of researching is following the trail where it leads you and expanding your knowledge along the way but it is important to stick to the trail and not be tempted down a different path.

2. The 'record office bore' (the real reason why you are not allowed to take sharp implements into the record office with you). This is probably a much worse distraction because you have less control over this one. The record office bore wants to tell you all about his (or her) researches in excruciatingly minute detail. It is the equivalent of being stuck next to the reality-challenged individual on the bus who wants to show you their photographs of electricity sub-stations, only less interesting. As we have been exposed from an early age to the culture of British politeness we will often find it very hard to be rude to such people who monopolise our time in such a self-centred fashion, and being rude is probably the only way to shut them up. As a result we can find ourselves stuck in the situation where our precious record office time is being eaten away by them and we cannot get away. Don't expect too much help from the record office staff – they are probably only too pleased that someone else is the victim instead of them.

We are not suggesting that you draw up a rigid schedule for your visit, work like a maniac and refuse to communicate with your fellow human beings. Rather we would suggest that you need to plan ahead, know what you want to find out, know which records to look in and make sure the office has those records available. You want to be able to focus on the task in hand and not waste the limited time available by being distracted for no good reason. After all, it is your time involved, and if you wish to achieve certain goals, and you have travelled for many miles to get there, it is not a good idea to be deflected away. How frustrating would it be to have to pay another visit to that office, just because you ran out of time and could only consult half of the series of parish burials for the village your family came from and needed to look at the other half to complete your mission?

> **Toni's tip:** It is a good idea to allow some time in your plan to look at the index cards and other indexed records. Although this is not targeted searching, indexes are usually quick and easy to use and can often lead to new lines of enquiry – ones which you would have never know about if the index hadn't led you to it.

And regarding the record office bore, prevention is better than cure. If you think you are being approached by one, don't look up, don't make eye contact and if you are spoken to, only answer questions monosyllabically or with a grunt – if you answer at all. If you are a reasonable speaker of another language – preferably something obscure in the UK like Kazakhstani – use that instead of English. Naturally you need to take notice of what they are saying, just in case it's something like 'are you aware your trousers are on fire' but never, ever, engage them in conversation unless you are prepared to lose the next two hours to them.

BEHIND EVERY SOLUTION LIES A PROBLEM

Anomalies, interpreting results and solving problems

"I appreciate that doing family history is like being a detective, but can we lose the bloodhound?"

Trap 30. The lines get tangled

Religion was taken much more seriously a few generations ago in Britain, with often very literal acceptance of the Christian expectation to go forth and multiply. Times were hard, with long hours of work and then this additional burden on top of everything else.

When a family has been successful in their attempts to procreate for a number of generations, and remain in the same area, there is a resulting build up of families that share the same surname. Unfortunately, they often recycle the same old first names, and this can cause difficulties in deciding which children belong to which branch of the family. First children were often named after the mother or father, and later children named after other family members, such as the father's favourite sister. There are exceptions, of course, but the majority of people were quite conservative over their choice of names for their offspring.

Take a man called John Barker, whose brothers were called William and James. John could have married an Ann and had children called John, Ann, William and James; William might marry an Eliza and have William, Eliza, John, and James; James might marry another Ann and have James, Ann, William and John. So in just two generations you could have four John, four James, four William, two Eliza and four Ann Barkers, with the children born roughly around the same time, not including any early children who did not survive. They often lived close to each other, and with a relatively common surname such as Barker, there could easily be other, unrelated Barker families nearby who may also use these names. Trying to separate out which particular Barker is your direct ancestor could be quite problematic.

Another common complication within the same family was the re-use of first names. Very often, if a child died, a later child was given the same name, so you could, for instance, get three sons called William born to a family, with only the latter one surviving childhood.

Lucky people have ancestors with names like Hephzibah. We hit a genealogical jackpot once when we found a mother who had called two of her children Augustus Nero and Cassebelian, but sadly names like these are very exceptional. Spare a thought for the genealogists of the future who will have to sort out the popular names of today, such as Lee or Jordan.

To avoid claiming the wrong set of ancestors as your own, you may have to untangle your direct line from a host of 'red herrings.' The ease of sorting out families like the Barkers above is dependent on other sources of information you can draw on, such as the census, which can help you sort out which child belongs to which parents. As you go back further in time, however, it becomes more difficult to be certain as you have a lesser number of secondary sources to help verify your deductions.

> **Toni's tip:** Try to identify all the matching families on the census, not just your direct line. This will help you be more certain that you have assigned the correct children to the right parents.

Here are some suggestions of things you can do to help sort out which child goes with which parent:

- Do the mathematics! In times gone by, couples would regularly produce children every 18 months to two years. If you find a child five months after the last one this is an indication you have assigned a wrong child to the couple. Be careful, though, not to rely on baptism dates as you cannot guarantee baptisms were carried out immediately after the birth of the child. Sometimes the parents would wait a couple of years before baptism - we have even seen offspring being baptised at the age of 25 or more!
- See if there are any Bishops' Transcripts available as a second check to an unclear Parish Register entry. They may also include different or additional information to that shown in the Parish Registers.
- You might be able to establish a family link by looking at the witnesses on a marriage certificate, as witnesses could be a relative, such as a sister.
- Follow each of the children you are trying to place in your tree forward in time on the census. You might find them in later life with a sibling, parent or niece/nephew living with them.
- After civil registration in 1837, obtaining birth certificates will give the mother's maiden name, but this is of course the expensive option (after the September quarter of 1911, the civil registration birth indexes show the mother's maiden surname, which may be sufficient to avoid buying the certificate just for this purpose).
- See how old the mother is. If she is older than 50 then she is unlikely to have given birth, although this is not completely impossible.

- Look for middle names as these can help. Sometimes the middle names used are the maiden surname of the mother. These middle names may be passed down through the generations until the origins are lost.
- Consider that the matching families may be related to one another, taking you back to a common set of ancestors.

Sometimes it just helps to write down your findings in a logical sequence, e.g. a timeline or put it into a table. This may help you fit pieces of the puzzle together or eliminate events that do not belong. This, however, did not help one newbie researcher that we are aware of. She was very confused with the number of households in a village where each head of household had one surname, but the rest of the family all had the surname 'Do'. It had to be gently pointed out to her that the 'Do' in this instance was a common abbreviation for the word 'Ditto.' Although Ditto is a surname in its own right, in this case, it just meant 'the same as above.'

"'Phone call for John Barker. Is there a John Barker here?"

Trap 31. They appear from nowhere

Once you have traced your family back beyond the census years, unless the family has remained in the same village for several hundred years, you may have a difficult time finding them. It is very common, when looking at parish records, for a single generation to seemingly pop up in the parish as if out of nowhere, have lots of children, then disappear as if they never ever existed. Parish records give you details on who was living there, but are not likely to tell you where they came from beforehand or where they moved to. You could be looking for someone who lived in the next-door village (about a mile away) who moved in after they got married and had their children there - or you could be looking for someone who was born in a different country. Without any kind of corroborative evidence, it is very difficult to establish a definite link between generations who move about the country.

Kate's comment: *Where you come from, a particular surname may be fairly uncommon, but in other parts of the country it might occur very frequently, so even if you have some evidence of where the family comes from, you need to take care that you have actually found the right one. To use the surname Fisher as an example, it is hardly ever found in Cornwall but is very common in Yorkshire and Lancashire. When you get an area of con-centration of a surname like this, it can indicate that this is the origin of that surname; that the first use of the name Fisher as a surname might have been in Yorkshire or Lancashire - although be careful, there is also a chance that this is not the case and the abundance of the name there might be down to one highly prolific family sometime in the past.*

Let us take a fictitious person, William Fisher, whose parents were John and Mary Fisher. We know that is the case because William was on the census giving his place of birth, and his baptism record from the parish church there shows that his parents were John and Mary. It can also be established from baptism records that John and Mary had another six children baptised in the village church. Unfortunately, however, there are no other birth, marriage or death records relating to John and Mary at that place.

So where did John and Mary come from? Where did they marry?

Where did they go? The surname Fisher is not particularly rare but it is not that common, either, so it might just be a case of looking for a marriage between a John Fisher and a Mary elsewhere in the country. However, a quick search of on-line resources shows that there are dozens of John Fishers marrying Marys - so which, if any, is the right one? Even if only one John Fisher and Mary marriage was found, it still could not be guaranteed to be the right one, because the records are incomplete and the one we are looking for may simply not be in existence or has not been digitised yet.

The answer then lies in finding corroborative evidence that the people you suspect as being 'yours' are indeed just that. Here are some ideas that you can pursue:

- Look at a map for the area around the parish where the earliest known record for your family occurs. Although people could relocate over considerable distances, most moves would be from a neighbouring village. Check adjacent counties, too, if your family's earliest known point of origin was close to a county border. You might be searching for Essex records in the west of the county but find your family moved a few miles from Hertfordshire into Essex.

- Check parish records to see if there was a John and Mary Fisher who lived nearby and who would fit the bill. You could establish this by seeing if they had children baptised at this other parish church, then suddenly stop having children there, and this ties in date-wise with the children baptised in the new parish. But check first that their disappearance from the original parish isn't simply that they died there.

- If you find John and Mary's death or burial records - do these tell you how old they were when they died? This can give you a date range in which they were likely to have married and had children.

- Check the parish records for the place where you know the family were living. Look for deaths or burials for any other children with the Fisher surname who were not baptised in that parish and see if you can find their baptisms showing John and Mary as parents. If you are lucky they may have unusual names like Obadiah or Lettice which will help you confirm the place they moved from.

- See if there is any paper trail showing a family's movement between parishes, such as a Settlement Examination or Removal Order. These were documents that proved a family's legal right to settle in a given area. Parish authorities were not keen on being lumbered with families that may become a financial burden and often sought to remove them elsewhere, which could include an indication of parish of origin.

- Look for marriages for potential earlier children in the new parish. Then look to see if they appear on censuses to see where they were born. If they are John and Mary's children they could point to the parish where John and Mary came from.
- Witnesses to the m arriages of John and Mary's children could be previously unknown relatives, which may give you a clue. You could also follow each of the children through the census to see if they ever have a cousin, aunt or uncle recorded as visiting them.
- See if there are any wills belonging to the family. These may mention relatives living in other parts of the country.
- Look for unusual middle names which might point at a mother's or grandmother's maiden surname.

All these actions may give you a theory that you can seek to prove or disprove, but how much corroborative evidence it takes to satisfy you that you have made the link is a personal thing. Rest assured, people have to come from somewhere – with the possible exception of Mr & Mrs Heypresto of Upper Sleevey.

Trap 32. What you were told doesn't fit

There is an old, oft-repeated story which illustrates the pitfalls of how words may get distorted as they are passed from person to person. The details vary but hinge around the idea that on a World War 1 battlefield, messages were passed through the trenches from person to person, each whispering what he had heard from the previous person. It is said that one message originated as "Send reinforcements. We are going to advance", but by the time it had reached the end of the line, it had transmuted into "Send three and fourpence. We are going to a dance." If this is true, it probably didn't produce the result that was originally hoped for.

Families may often be rich in stories but invariably as these stories and information pass through a family they are subject to distortions and interpretations which alter the facts. This happens by accident but unfortunately once the distorted words are presented as facts, they are firmly believed and it can be difficult to convince the person 'at the end of the line' that what they understand as truth is a distortion.

Naturally, any story handed down through the family is worth further research to see if there is some truth there.

Toni was told that one of her great-grandfathers was a sea captain. As the evidence pointed to the family being of humble stock, this did not seem to fit easily as the rank of sea captain sounds quite grand. When Toni followed the ancestor in question on later censuses, he was variously a night watchman or a dock labourer, not quite what had been predicted. Going back in time, however, revealed that he was a mariner who had achieved the rank of Able Seaman but there was no evidence of anything higher than that.

You could have been told that your great grandfather was a publican. On consulting each census you find he had a veritable cornucopia of jobs: a news vendor; labourer; sugar baker; night watchman; and sewer man. A trade directory may reveal him as the land-lord of the Saucy Nancy public house for four years between 1874 and 1878. So he was a publican - but only for a short while and had many other occupations during his lifetime. This goes to show that ten years between censuses is a long time, and unskilled people often changed their occupations and had to take whatever job was on offer.

It may be a family fact that you are from good, Northern stock, your forebears working in the Lancashire mills for generations and were all hardy, clog and flat cap-wearing, beer-swigging cricket players with their whippets kept on a piece of string - and that was just the women. Stories weave their way through your family which say how great-great uncle Albert, aged six, lost his ears in a freak accident with an early example of Arkwright's Spinning Jenny and how he was never able to wear a flat cap again. Your heritage couldn't be more Lancastrian if it tried. However, your family history researches may tell a different story. You could discover that your roots were in fact in Suffolk. Your forebears might have formed part of the migration that took poor, often agricultural workers, from rural areas to the northern mills. Agents would visit workhouses and the like with promises of assisted passage and work. So instead of being gritty Northerners, you are in fact Southern, shandy-drinking wusses.

That research may not tally with a family fact can be illustrated with a genuine story about a family from Norfolk for whom we carried out some investigations. Their family story was about an ancestor called Charlie Martins who left Norfolk with a friend to seek their fortune in London. Charlie did not do so well, but his friend made good. The story indicated that the friend's surname was Colman, and he later went on to form the Colman mustard business.

It is a really interesting story, and research of the records revealed that Charlie Martins did exist (he was the two-times great grandfather of the person we were doing the research for). It was also established that he moved to London. Sadly, there was no evidence of anyone called Colman in Charlie's household or surrounding area on the censuses. What is more, the history and expansion of the Colman mustard business pre-dated Charlie's move to London. So these findings seemed to throw doubt on the tale.

However, earlier in time, the Martins family were close neigh bours and in all likelihood friends with the Dix family. The Dix and Martins families lived in Stoke Holy Cross, near to the Mill where the Colman family first produced their mustard. There is also evidence that members of the Dix family worked for Colman's. Additionally, one Dix family member, also called Charlie and a near contemporary of Charlie Martins, started his own mustard making business in Norfolk.

So in all probability, there was something behind the family story. Charlie Dix and Charlie Martins were likely to be the two friends referred to in the story. It looks like Charlie Martins went to London and did not make good, whereas his friend Charlie Dix stayed behind and did well for himself. But the entire Martins family story about Charlie and his friend going to London to seek their fortune does not, as the saying goes, cut the mustard.

Kate's comment: If you discover that the details you are uncovering do not fit what you have been told as 'gospel' by the family, there is always the possibility that you have made a mistake and are following the wrong family. You might need to go back and reconsider all the links to make sure you are following the right line. Alternatively, the family story may be basically correct but attached to the wrong person - instead of part of the direct line, it might be for a distant cousin. The other option, too, might be that the person giving you the stories just has a very powerful imagination . . .

Trap 33. You don't flesh out the facts

One of the great things about family history is that you don't know before you start where it will take you. As we have said, the stories that attach to a family are important, but some are very hard to prove. One such example is about a friend of Kate's who wanted to know more about her grandfather. She knew he was Jewish and the family story was that in 1944 he had been run over by a tram in Holland, where he had been living. Now a simple consideration of events in Europe at that time indicated that a Jewish man in Holland in 1944 probably had a different, more unpleasant fate and this story was probably wrong. She felt that she had been given this story as a child to shelter her from the probable reality so she tried looking on a website which lists the names of Holocaust victims, but he was not listed. No evidence of his death in Holland could be found, either. There was simply no corroborative evidence of his existence in Holland at all. Later, an elderly aunt disclosed what had really happened to him. He had been living in the UK and had become unwell and had been committed to a mental asylum, where he eventually died. The family had tried to cover up the perceived stigma of mental illness with an elaborate cover story.

Sometimes you cannot prove a story, but with a bit of digging around, it may be possible to find evidence which can lend it weight. Take one of Toni's family lines, the Sheals. The story in the family is that this line is of Scandinavian origins. Having traced the family back to the 1700s they all lived in Norfolk and most earned their living as fishermen. Their roots seem to be based in a coastal village by the name of Winterton on Sea. Not much evidence of Scandinavian origins so far.

Then about 20 years ago, Toni's father visited the village of Winterton on Sea and got into conversation with an elderly man who lived there and whose surname was Sheals. He too had been told that the family were of Scandinavian descent, and as Toni's strand of the family left the village almost 200 years ago, the likelihood is that this story has passed down the family from at least that time. This still not proof of Scandinavian origins but does show that the story has been in the family for a very long time.

Toni did some research on the surname itself, finding that in the past it co-existed in the same locality with families bearing the names Skeels or Skeales. These names have a more Scandinavian sound to them and there is evidence that the names Skeels or Shiels were from the same root and have Scandinavian origins. This implies a link, and given that Norfolk saw an influx of Vikings in the 7th Century, there is a possibility that the name might originate from their language. Perhaps DNA testing will be able to provide more concrete proof of the Sheals' origins in the future but at present, although looking probable, it is still a matter of conjecture.

> ***Toni's tip:*** *When looking to prove a story, first establish a timeframe in which the event was likely to have occurred – so that you can focus your search.*

Trap 34. You hit the brick wall

Getting frustrated with your researches may tempt you to hit your head against a brick wall, but in family history terms, 'hitting the brick wall' means something different. It is when you have reached what you believe to be a dead-end with tracing your family history and nothing you do seems to allow you to progress your researches beyond this point. Brick walls can appear at any stage, sometimes at the beginning of your journey. You are bound to run into a brick wall sooner or later, but the secret is to not give up as there may be things you can do to overcome it. Each case will have its own particular requirements but here are some suggestions that might help:

Your first step should be to revisit everything you have done so far. Check that there isn't some small scrap somewhere that first time round you have dismissed as irrelevant but could lead you onto the correct path. It could be something as simple as an unusual middle name for a child, or a witness on a marriage certificate. As you are going through your data, ensure that you can corroborate your findings. Have you made any mistakes?

Have you made assumptions that have led to your research parameters being too narrow?

It may help to widen dates or geographical areas to be searched. Instead of relying on transcripts, try to see the original documents or scanned images of the originals. A mistake in transcription might send you on completely the wrong path. If you had an ancestor who was born in Hadleigh, Suffolk, and the transcriber had said Hadleigh, Essex, you may well find no other evidence for the family in Essex and give up. A transcript, too, might not hold all the information that appears on the original document - there may be notes in the margins, or additional entries that have been overlooked.

If this does not help, then consider further work on surname variations. You might have already searched with variations of the spelling but have you thought sufficiently out of the box? For example, the name Sibbard has been recorded as Stiband. This is very different to the original and not an obvious choice to search under. Look to see if anyone has started a one-name study or start one yourself - although it is probably best to ignore this suggestion if the name you are looking for is Smith.

Try to attack the problem from a different angle. Follow the trail of known and suspected siblings or other family members, as sometimes details will emerge which will help you move on. They may reveal references to cousins, aunts or uncles, or a known relative may be lodging with a family that also turns out to be distantly related. A witness to a marriage may be the future spouse of the other witness, which may be valuable corroborative evidence. Look at records for all members of the family and friends, spouses, neighbours, and so on. Obtain wills, not just for people who are definitely on your family tree, but perhaps try speculative ones - people with the same surname, who live around the area your family were from, and especially those who may have a similar occupation, especially if it is an unusual one.

Kate's comment: *Take some quiet contemplation time and try to put yourself in the place of the ancestor concerned. Think how he or she may have left a paper trail. Did he have a trade like glassblowing? Could he have been an apprentice? Did he work for a company that still exists who might have old staff records in their archives?*

Try drawing up a conjectural tree using people you think might be related but you are not sure. Then try following these individuals in the hope that you can tie them in somewhere. Summarise your problem in writing, as this will help you spot any gaps or places you haven't yet looked in. This will also have an additional help in that if you put your researches away, when you pick them up again (and you probably will), you will know precisely what you have done and so will not repeat any of it.

Ask others for help. Seek the advice of another amateur family historian or professional genealogist and let them look through your research. They may spot something you have missed. Seek out anyone else who is researching the family, make contact and see whether they have anything or know anything that you don't. If you follow this route, be careful, as not everyone else's research is going to meet your standards, so be sure to check anything they give to you.

> ***Toni's tip:*** *Talk through your problem to a friend or the dog. It is amazing how often to talk out loud gives you a new perspective – probably because you have to précis the problem in a logical sequence, and it helps you realise there are gaps or other things to try. And the dog won't mind, although the friend might.*

If all else fails, put your research to one side, concentrate on another line then go back to it later with fresh eyes. You might have developed new ideas or skills or there may be new records or indexes available for you to search.

Trap 35. You take it as fact

It would be really awful to dedicate a huge chunk of your life to drawing up your family history for your surname, only to find out on your mother's death bed that you were conceived whilst the person you thought of as Dad was away on business and therefore had no genetic link to the name. At the same time you find out why the butcher always gave your mum a cheery wink and slipped an extra sausage or two into her order.

You may have started out doing all the right things: interviewing the family; gathering all their information; going back to the great grandparents; and drawing up a rudimentary family tree which you take as your starting point for research. Your tree might be growing nicely but it could be completely wrong. Your great-grandfather might not be your bloodline at all, he could be a step-great grandfather. Your grandfather might have taken on his surname when his mother remarried and your grandfather's real surname was thus airbrushed out of history. You should check the details, starting with yourself. Can you be sure your parents are telling you the truth about your origins? We know of families today where the youngest child has grown up thinking that their older sister is just that, but she is really the child's mother, and the people thought of as parents are, in fact, the grandparents.

> **Toni's tip:** *Remember though that not everything written down is fact – many a child will have a father shown on a certificate who is not the biological father. DNA tests can sometimes unwittingly bring this to light – it is known as a non-paternity event.*

The moral of this tale is that you should always seek out corroborative evidence. But what is acceptable corroborative evidence and how much do you need? This is up to you but as a general rule most people look for three pieces of evidence. For example, if you are looking for your great grandfather's birth, we might find him in the Civil Registration records and order the birth certificate which would name his parents; we may also find him in the baptism registers which would also confirm his parents; and also find him on at least one census record with his parents for the third piece of evidence. If he lived through the census era we might find him with his parents on more than one census, and other miscellaneous records such as his father's military record. So it is possible to end up with 5, 6 or more pieces of evidence to prove the fact. Unfortunately, pre-1841 you are unlikely to find as much evidence to corroborate your findings and will probably have to satisfy yourself with less. If you are not convinced, you can draw up a conjectural tree, with a view to seeking out further evidence at a later date.

> **Kate's comment:** *When people are trying to prove a genealogical link through DNA testing, and a non-paternity event has occurred, the results will be skewed. It could lead you to erroneously believe that two strands of a family with the same surname have different origins. Even if you suspect this to be the case, you are unlikely to be able to determine whether the event occurred, say, one or ten generations back, so you will be none the wiser.*

If there is a single piece of evidence without corroboration, it is up to you to decide whether it is enough or not for your family tree. You don't have to stand up in court to swear that you are correct, but it may mean there are mistakes if you accept evidence at face value. For your own satisfaction, you really should strive to set a standard of proof which is acceptable. Perhaps you could adopt a court system idea, so for ancestors during the census era, you should look for "beyond reasonable doubt" and for the pre-census era you might accept "balance of probability."

"Can you confirm that this is the sausage that led you to believe your wife was having an affair?"

Trap 36. You suffer from information overload

Alexander Pope wrote: "A little knowledge is a dangerous thing." Albert Einstein built on that: "A little knowledge is a dangerous thing. So is a lot." His wasn't an original thought, as a biblical passage has Festus telling Paul that 'too much learning would drive you mad.' He certainly had a point. We are bombarded with so much information, via our computers, newspapers, televisions, radios, mobile phones and so on that if we were to retain all this new information we would probably forget useful stuff like how to walk or chew. A recent article in the Daily Telegraph asserted that British workers have to sift through so many emails and electronic documents that the equivalent of two weeks a year are wasted just on searching for information that has been previously read then lost.

There is a parallel here with your family history data. Even if you have only been researching for a short while, you can build up a colossal quantity of data in various forms, such as in an electronic database; files of original documentation such as certificates, family letters and photographs; notebooks containing information written on visits to record offices; printed information off the Internet, and so on, and you cannot possibly remember it all. So what do you do when you are looking for a particular piece of information but you aren't sure whereabouts you have seen it in your ever-expanding archive? It might be something straightforward like trying to prove that two people are one and the same person, and you know you have seen a reference to an occupation which might help establish this, and all you need to do is find it.

Ordering your data in some kind of logical sequence will make finding things simpler. This can be done how it best suits you - it could be by name, geographical area, or family group. Certificates and similar documents could be kept in date order or alphabetically or you could have one section for every person and everything relating to that person is kept in there.

There are established numbering systems developed by genealogists where each individual in a family is allocated a number and this is indexed. Any data pertaining to that individual will be annotated with that number. The most well-known of these is the Ahnentafel system, (from German, meaning 'ancestor table.') This starts with a base point, such as yourself, which has the number 1. Your father would be given number 2, your mother 3, your father's father 4, father's mother 5, mother's father 6, and so on. You can adapt it to give children a sub-section number, so your mother's eldest sister, your Aunt Lucy, would be 3(i), her brother 3(ii).

It is good practice periodically to read through all of your collected data, including examining photographs. As your knowledge of the family expands you might be able to establish links and discover new routes for exploration which you couldn't do in earlier times. You might, for example, be able to establish that someone with your surname whom you could not previously slot in to your tree is in fact a second cousin, simply because you have been able to gather more data on your cousins.

You can also get too close to a subject. You could spend all day sifting through masses of information trying to establish a connection but you can't make it happen. It is worth trying to leave the task for the next day or week, then when you come back with fresh eyes you may instantly find the connection.

> **Toni's tip:** *It is also useful to have a list of things yet to be followed up, or what to do next – and this will save you time when you next pick up your family history.*

Do try to be selective over what you keep in your files and limit it to items that are relevant to your particular family. Whilst it is always good to read around and get a flavour of what life was like for your forebears, you don't need to catalogue every last item of historical interest. Just because great-grandfather worked on a farm, this doesn't mean you need to hold onto a complete set of Pig Breeder Monthly magazines.

Trap 37. You have extra pieces of the puzzle

A parallel could be drawn between slotting all the bits of evidence you have gathered together to complete a family tree, and the art of jigsaw puzzle completion. In fact, if you were to create a Venn diagram of family history lovers and jigsaw puzzle completers, we suspect you would get a considerable overlap. With your family history, you are probably aiming to achieve the equivalent of a completed 10,000 piece jigsaw puzzle of the Tower of London, but in reality you are more likely to have 1,200 pieces of the Tower of London plus 35 pieces of the Empire State building, 17 pieces of a Tyrannosaurus rex and a bit of a cute Labrador puppy.

It's a bit of a balancing act, knowing how much information and what information to collect as you go along. Whilst it is not a good idea to have masses of irrelevant facts, there is always the danger that you if don't keep something, it might later turn out to be relevant. However, you don't have it any more and don't know where you got it from. So what do you do? Do you collect lots of information and hope to sort it out later or do you only record what you know for definite to be of relevance to you?

Most of us will have collected bits of information which we think may belong to our family, but have no idea where they will fit in. They will be shoved in a file (or files) or stacked on a desk waiting to be sorted out. The larger the pile, the less chance you stand of making any kind of sensible order of it and useful things will be lost in the jumble.

A suggestion is to keep a spreadsheet or table and to enter each piece of miscellaneous data into this. This could have columns for name, time period it refers to, the source, plus notes which may detail, for example, any connections made to other data or what needs to be done to follow this up. Each item could have an identification number that can be cross-referenced into the notes column. This might seem like a lot of effort but it will give you an easily reviewed précis of all your floating bits of paper and what further research needs to be done.

Toni's tip: When you are trying to assign your miscellaneous data to individuals, don't just concentrate on trying to make links to the direct line. Look at siblings and other members of the wider family. If you don't, you may be reducing your chances of incorporating something interesting into your family tree. If you can make these links, you can derive enormous satisfaction, especially if the connection takes you away from your line of unexciting agricultural labourers and into new territories.

Of course, the downside of spending time on speculative research is that you might find that after all your effort this person or event has absolutely nothing to do with your family. This can be very disappointing. However, imagine your satisfaction if it turns out that you really are related to the gentleman who won a pie eating contest in 1823. . .

Trap 38. You ignore your inner voice

Do you have a hunch? We are talking about that feeling in your bones that keeps nagging away at you, not the possibility of you adopting the role of Quasimodo for the local Amateur Dramatic society. Police officers might refer to this phenomenon as having a nose for trouble, or antique dealers may refer to a buzz or vibration they feel when they find something which later turns out to be very valuable. It could be described as a sixth sense, an instinct or intuition that draws you in a particular direction.

Genealogists too may experience this inner voice which is trying to tell you something. There is a lot to be said for listening and following this inner voice, unless it is of the sort that tells you that you are Genghis Khan and that you really should acquire an empire through the medium of bloody warfare. It's probably best to ignore that particular voice.

There isn't always a great deal of logic to it, and no explanation as to why you get this feeling. You can be drawn to a particular record or entry, even though there are matches that are closer to the information that you already hold. Sometimes this sixth sense is helpful and leads you to the person you want. Sometimes it isn't helpful, but if you ignore it, you might be missing the opportunity to find the link that has been so elusive up to that point.

The following example shows how illogical yet how effective following your hunch can be. Toni was trying to track down a very elusive person. She had found him with certainty on the 1901 census for Grays, Essex. The entry gave the following details:

Denis Edwin Turner, Dock Labourer, born about 1863
Maidstone, Kent

A matching Denis Edwin Turner could not be found on any of the three previous censuses, and even allowing for mis-indexing and/or missing records, this was not usual. However, Toni had a very strong feeling that the following entry in Poplar, Middlesex, on the 1881 census was of interest, even though the person concerned did not share the same first name, surname, occupation, date of birth and town of birth with Denis, in fact, not a lot in common:

Edwin Tanner, General Labourer, born about 1861 Linton, Kent

Information from the Tanner family indicated that they thought there could have been a change of surname in the family from Turner, but there were other 1881 entries that more closely matched the one on the 1901 census. Logically this one did not fit well but Toni had a very strong hunch about this one, so she printed and filed the entry for later consideration. This was a good move as later on, corroborative evidence came about which showed that Edwin Tanner and Denis Turner were in fact one and the same person.

Why was Toni drawn to this entry? Is it some strange force that we are only vaguely aware of, perhaps our ancestors placing ideas and thoughts into our subconscious minds ... or did Toni just strike it lucky?

Who knows? Of course it is not good practice to accept just the one you get the gut feeling for, unless you can later find very good corroborative evidence. As Gil Grissom (of the American forensic television drama C.S.I.) once said: "Always believe .... always verify." Accept that your inner voice could mislead you and if you believe it unquestioningly you might end up trying to make facts fit your hunch, rather than looking for the right evidence in the first place.

Why Denis Turner changed his name is not known. One possibility is that Turner may be the name of his biological father, however, there could be more devious reasons. His descendants, however, thought that he changed his name to avoid the interest of the law as he had committed a serious crime. We will probably never find out the true reason but if it was to escape the law then he had succeeded, but he didn't manage to escape the genealogists!

Toni's tip: *If your inner voice is telling you something is wrong with a finding - even if it is the only option – don't ignore it. There may be a good reason behind it, but one that you can't quite put your finger on. Try to prove or disprove the validity of the entry before accepting it. Don't get too hung up on this - if you are getting negative thoughts about an entry then you should look at it but don't let it put you into a negative mindset that does not allow you to accept the results of your researches, just because you don't feel they are right.*

The subconscious mind is a powerful tool. Sometimes just going to sleep on a problem allows you to wake up the next day with a solution fully formed - somehow, whilst you slept, part of your mind has worked over the problem and sorted it out. You might not remember it consciously, but perhaps your 'hunch' is a dim memory of something you have read or have been told about. Whatever the explanation, remember to take heed of those little inner voices.

Trap 39. Too much effort – too little payback

The genealogist as a Bull Terrier is not a metaphor that readily springs to mind, but the thing both creatures have in common is that once they get their teeth into something, very little can be done to prize their jaws off until they decide they want to let go. No family historian worth their salt wants to let go of a problem or retire defeated from a brick wall. They will always have this in their mind and will try again and again to find that one piece of evidence that will help solve the mystery. But once the historian has licked the face of, chewed on each limb and then sunk their teeth into the buttocks of the problem, metaphorically speaking, there are not many places left for them to go.

"If he starts to mount your leg, just hit him with a rolled up copy of Family History Weekly"

When you first start doing your family history, the whole process is very exciting and interesting, and you are able to reap a fair amount of reward for the amount of input you give. You find it fairly easy and quick to get a lot of information, but as time goes by, the amount of work you put in may stay constant but the quantity of information you get back decreases. As you get less reward for your effort, the later stages of your family history researches become less interesting and may become a bit of a slog. At this point, most people will consider that they have gone as far as they can, because they have become tired of the whole process.

So when you have read and re-read your old information, talked to relatives again, tried other researchers, used message boards and blogs, come at the problem from all angles and spent many, many hours on the problem, and all you are doing is going over the same old areas, then is the time to say enough is enough? The answer is probably yes, but just for a while. It could just be that you need an interlude to give your mind time to rest. A new day can bring you new theories, and you can approach the problem at a later time with renewed interest and enthusiasm.

Toni reached that point with the Neobard line some 30 years ago. The whole process had been very interesting but it then started to become a bit of a slog, as she had at the latter stages spent days in record offices looking for new details, but without success. She had traced back to a Samuel Nevard or Nebard, who appears at the top of her tree but she could get no further. Toni has established that Samuel was born around 1687, his wife was called Catherine, and they settled and had their children in Eye, Suffolk. But his village of origin has not been established, despite there being some strong contenders. Similarly, a place of marriage for the couple is not known. A manual check of parish registers for the surrounding villages has not yielded results, nor has increasing the size of the search circle around Eye.

Toni even undertook a one-name study, piecing together everyone with the surname or variant thereof. Although her knowledge of this family grew immensely, this process did not crack her problem.

From time to time, Toni reviews her family history, and has another look at this line just to see if any new records have been released which might help her with those elusive early Neobards. During these revisits, she has looked at newly released records. She has also looked at the problem from different angles, including developing theories linking Samuel and Catherine to other families, and then sought to prove a link, but to no avail. During another of these periodic revisits, Toni pursued the idea that the couple's three children called Jonathan (the first two of which had died in infancy) were named after another family member. As the name Jonathan clearly had significance in the family, it was possible that it could have belonged to the boys' paternal grandfather. Sadly despite best efforts, this could not be proved. However, she remains forever optimistic that one day her wall will be bulldozed.

TELLING IT LIKE IT IS

Presenting and Disseminating Your Family History

"Whilst I know you believed they were all in trade,
you were partially correct. Unfortunately, their
trade was blackmail, fraud and prostitution.
On the bright side, they were all working..."

Trap 40. You keep it all to yourself

Some people are not naturally inclined towards sharing. History shows us that from time to time, true philanthropists have given so generously of their time and fortunes that they have changed the face of the world. Others have been less inclined to part with even a small bit of themselves. Take, for instance, one particularly stingy person, Hetty Green, who in 1864 inherited a 5.7 million dollar fortune; today this would be worth around 110 million. Most of us would be delighted with this sum, but not our Hetty. In an attempt to increase her wealth yet further, she alienated her relatives by challenging the will of a wealthy aunt, to the extent that she was accused of forgery. She reputedly did not change her underwear until the current lot had worn out; never used hot water and on one occasion was said to have spent many hours searching through her carriage for a dropped 2 cent stamp. Her lack of largesse extended to her children – when her son broke his leg, she tried to get him treated in a free clinic. Ultimately, he lost his leg and had a prosthetic one (made from cork). When she died, she had managed to squirrel away around 200 million dollars. No doubt she would not have approved that her son married a Texan prostitute and spent part of his mother's inheritance on, amongst other things, a diamond encrusted chamber pot.

As a family historian, you might not think it is important to share your family history. This may not necessarily be because you are inherently mean. It could be as simple as not having enough time or you might not realise that others would be interested, but for a number of reasons it would be a shame to keep it to yourself.

For example, if anything happened to you, what happens to your research? Even if you take the trouble to keep it in a database this does not mean it is left in a readily understandable form. Worse still, if you keep it all in your head, there is no hope that anyone could access it in the event of anything unfortunate befalling you. You will also be missing the opportunity to derive pleasure from sharing it with other family members, who may be equally enthralled and delighted with what you have found.

If your relatives have shared family documents or stories with you, then showing them the finished result of your researches is a way of returning the compliment. If you share with the wider family then you may trigger memories which could result in more family stories, information, documents, or photographs coming your way.

"I was hoping to find out about Great Auntie Maud but all I seem to be getting are re-runs of Coronation Street."

When you decide now is the time to share, you will need to consider the medium by which you will share this information. A database is, of course, a fantastic tool and if you have diligently recorded everything onto it, it will really help with your research. However, it is not necessarily the best method of presenting your family history to others. Most family history database programmes are capable of producing various family trees and reports, but on their own these can be hard to read and a little uninspiring.

It will help if you consider your potential audience and make sure that whatever you produce is appropriate for them. For example, if you have a number of family members who perhaps are not adept at using computers then you might want to produce your research as a book or assembled in a folder.

If you decide to write up your family history in book form, you can find plenty of guidance to help you with this task. It is quite a time-consuming task and may be harder to do than you imagine. It also could be costly but if you have the time and resources this is a lovely thing to achieve. Alternatively, if your ambitions do not run to this, then producing a scrap book of your researches can be fun and informative without the associated costs.

If you have relatives living abroad, you may want to consider publishing your research as a website. A website has the advantage of making your research available to a wider audience and perhaps to make links with unknown family in different parts of the world.

> *Toni's tip:* When writing up your family history, work from the assumption that the reader will know nothing. You may run the risk of falling foul of stating the obvious but you will be assured that you have made everything clear for your readers - including ones that are not even born yet! A good clear record of your family history can in itself become a family heirloom, passed down through the generations after you are long gone.

So really, there is nothing to stop you getting underway with plans for sharing the fruits of your labour. Nothing, that is, apart from child-care, work, sleep, decorating, shopping, cleaning, mowing the lawn, feeding the dog, putting the rubbish out, washing and ironing, having fun . . .

Trap 41. I'll share it when I've finished it

Eureka! The now fabled word of the genius Archimedes as he worked out his theory of displacement whilst in the bath. According to the story, he leapt out of the bath and ran home naked to put the final touches to his theory so he could share it with the world. It's a good job that when as he emerged from the bath he didn't tread on the soap, fall over, bash his head and spend the rest of his days weaving baskets. Otherwise how long would we have had to wait before another mathematical genius came along? (NB if you are a keen mathematician, this is a rhetorical question, please don't give us the probabilities of this happening).

This should be taken as a salutary warning. Archimedes, of course, had a burning desire to share his genius with the world. If you are waiting until you have finished your family history before sharing it with anyone; or if you are saying that you will be ready to share soon, but just want to tie up a few loose ends first – beware. The truth is that you will never, ever, finish. Family history can be likened to the labours of Sisyphus. In Greek mythology, he was made to roll a huge boulder up a steep hill, and before he could reach the top the massive stone would always roll back down, forcing him to begin again. So too, the family historian – just when you think you have reached the peak of your endeavours, you find another area that needs to be investigated.

As well as never having a finished product, the longer you go on with your family researches, the more information you will have. You could end up with boxes full of unsorted photographs, letters, certificates and diaries which may take another ten years just to sort out! The prospect of doing all this could become overwhelming and you may feel completely daunted by the task.

You could opt for the middle ground, where you do not go for full-on book production and publication, but instead arrange the material in a loose-leaf folder or similar and tell the story of your researches up to that moment. You will probably have to produce further folders as the story unfolds. By sharing your findings to date, you may encourage useful feedback and have new leads generated, especially with those elderly relatives who are still amongst us.

If you haven't got sufficient time even for this, then you could consider collaborating with another family member (or members). There may be someone who does not have family history skills but is willing and able to sort out the information into a presentable package on your behalf.

> *Toni's tip:* *If you have a big family, perhaps spread in different places in the world, you could consider issuing, say, a 6 monthly newsletter where you update your research, and encourage other family members to send you articles about themselves and their families. This way you keep up to date with hatches, matches and dispatches! But make sure that the recipients actually want to get it!*

"Mum, the family history newsletter is here"

If you are still reluctant to share, then perhaps you are just a procrastinator. Remember, there is no time like the present, and you are probably not going to feel any more enthusiastic about the effort in sharing next year than you are now. Eventually you will run out of reasons why you shouldn't start – after all, you now have sufficient stocks of vellum; the common cold has been cured, world peace is assured, and Capricorn is rising in the house of Aries, so how about knuckling down and getting on with it!

Trap 42. Publishing a book is beyond your reach

It is said that we all have a book inside us. No doubt when publishers receive some of these masterpieces from hopeful authors, they wish that they had been kept inside. To you, of course, your family history is fascinating and exciting, and it defeats you as to why complete strangers wouldn't find your work a 'page turner.' But the sad fact is that most family histories are of interest just to that particular family, unless you are descended from someone famous or notorious, such as a well known actor or a serial killer. Some people have managed to get a publisher interested in their work but as a general rule you will be wasting your time trying to get a mainstream readership for your family history.

You may have a driving need to write a book and have it profession-ally printed. The motivations for this may vary. For many it is about leaving something tangible behind for future generations so that the information that has been carefully collected and collated is not forgotten about. A route to doing this is to publish your material yourself.

To self-publish is a bit of a minefield and can be very expensive. For many this will not be an option, and you should be very wary of vanity publishers, who promise a lot but deliver very little at great expense to you. A genuine publisher may well want to charge you for aspects of their services, but will discriminate as they only wish to publish books that will sell. Vanity publishers are more than happy to get anyone to part with their money and they have very little interest in the book actually selling, so saleability and quality of the work do not rank highly in their priorities. They may well expect you to pay for a minimum print run of hundreds or even thousands of books when all you really need are about 10. So rather than pursue a publisher, vanity or otherwise, to put your work into print, there are other options that you might like to consider.

If you are prepared to put in all the hard work yourself, you can write and design your book, including the layout, and submit this to a 'print on demand' service. You will need to supply a digital file of your book to the printer or publishing service who will then print a copy whenever one is requested. This avoids the need for costly large print runs and means that you have the facility to have copies to give to family and friends (or get them to pay for their own). Some companies allow you to design your own cover and upload your manuscript, whereas others offer to lay out your book and design a cover for you. The latter are likely to charge for these services. The benefit of using an on-demand service is that it can be cheaper than using your own home printer, the turn-around time can be quite fast and your manuscript will be produced in a proper book format. The downside is that your options may be quite limited in some respects by the services your publisher offers, such as choice of colours or you may not be able to incorporate photographs. It pays to look around and compare what is available from different organisations.

> *Toni's tip:* If you have something interesting to say consider submitting an article to a national magazine or a family history society journal. They will always consider a well-written piece which will have an appeal to a wide readership. Such articles may often generate feedback that can help you further with your family history research.

If a whole book seems beyond your reach or you aren't that bothered by the idea, then you could perhaps consider other ways to create a professional-looking record of your family history. You could, for example, put together a book of photographs. Free software is readily available on the internet which allows you to scan your old photographs and create a photo album together with captions and titles. You may wish include a foreword and acknowledgements. These can then be printed for a reasonable cost with either a hard cover (together with dust jackets) or with a soft cover.

Another option to consider is using your family photographs to make a unique calendar for your family, either a wall, desktop or poster-style calendar. They could make interesting and unusual birthday or Christmas presents for your relatives. There are a number of on-line sites which can do this for you relatively cheaply and are quite straightforward to use.

"I've never seen Great Auntie Maud
quite like that before."

Trap 43. Your website was an expensive folly

It doesn't seem to matter how much money and expertise is thrown at creating some websites, they still manage spectacularly to not achieve the purpose they were designed for. People who tried to buy tickets for the London 2012 Olympics when the website first opened were greeted with the following message: "Sorry, we cannot process your request at this time." Notwithstanding the designers' best efforts, the website could not cope with the volume of requests for the 2.3 million tickets on offer, and just ground to a halt.

Whilst the creation of a website to share your family history is not going to be as complex or expensive as creating the Olympic ticket website, the opportunity to get it wrong still exists. It is worth considering this method, however, as it is a very good way of publishing information at a relatively low cost (provided you are sensible about it). It is very useful for relatives that live a long way away, and may also provide a method whereby previously unknown people who have a link to your family may discover you. A website also has a big advantage over a printed book in that you can update a website as often as you want or as new information emerges.

You don't have to be very technically minded or rich in order to set up an effective website. There are free tools around that allow those of us with Luddite tendencies to set up a simple site and to maintain it with little effort. The only skill you really need is to be able to use basic word processing software. Many packages offer you ready-made colour schemes and themes to choose from. There will be guides and tutorials available to guide you through the process, or you might be able to find free or reasonably low cost courses locally that can teach you what to do.

Of course there are costs involved. You will need a website name, which is also called a domain name. This needs to be unique, and preferably something simple. You will need to register it so that it becomes your domain name and cannot be used by anyone else, and the registration will involve a small set up fee and an annual fee to keep it. You may also need to pay a hosting fee. This is to a service provider who will store your data (such as images and files) from where it can be accessed by the users. Often the registering of the domain name and the hosting can be through the same company.

When you are setting up your website, you will need to consider what the focus of your website is. Typically, it will be around your surname but think how you are going to break down the information you will show. You could organise your information into topics, such as 'family trees'; 'occupations' and 'places lived'. The more simple and logical the format, the easier it will be to use and the more people you will attract to use it.

> **Kate's comment:** *A quick look on the Internet at other people's family history websites will show you exactly what we mean. Some websites just present their data in long lists without any kind of organisation and it can be annoying and frustrating trying to battle your way through this. Have a browse through a few - if you find a format you like, design something similar for your site.*

Generally the hosting organisation will limit the amount of space available for your website. If you need more space it may cost you more. It pays therefore to consider exactly what you want to upload. If you use a lot of images they will take up a lot of your hosting space and will probably be time-consuming to load. Consider the colour scheme you use, too - a livid pink and purple arrangement may look zingy and bright but after a while will be very tiresome to look at and may be slow to load. From a user's point of view, printing information from the website can use a lot of ink if, for example, if it is white text on a blue background. People can also be put off by flashing adverts and banners. Whilst it is fun to put bangs and whizzes into your website, they may not be so delightful for the reader.

You will also need to attract the right people to view your website, which will mean ensuring that when people want to find you, they can. There are procedures that you can adopt which makes your website more noticeable to a search engine. For example, if you change your text regularly, you are more likely to be listed in a search. The easiest way to ensure you have a regular change of text in your website is to host a blog. Make sure, too, that you invite people to contact you, and show an email address so that they can. They may have useful information to add to your website or researches, or might turn out to be long lost relatives!

> **Toni's tip:** *Look into search engine optimisation to ensure your website is prominent. You might have the best website in the world but if search engines do not pick it up then nobody will know it is there.*

Consider, too, the use of social media. If you can set up a link to a feed that relates to the name you have been researching, you will attract interest from a wider audience. A friend of us has set up a Facebook group for people within her family to share photographs, stories and any other related information on the family. It is a very active group and although it was not set up for family history purposes originally, it has generated a lot of material that would probably not easily have come to light.

A slight word of caution. If you are intending to publish a website for both lines of your parentage, ensure that the web name is not misleading. It is fine if you have Sampson and Curtis as your family names and thus your website address is www.sampsoncurtis.co.uk, but not so good if your family names are Large and Willey or Bigg and Bazookas. You just might find you attract a different sort of visitor to your site.

Trap 44. Your work is plagiarised

Who would have thought that beneath the respectable, genteel world of genealogy there lurks a seedy, cut-throat underworld of grasping, stealing historians who will stop at nothing to relieve you of your hard-won knowledge and ideas and to claim credit for your work. Such bare-faced thievery cannot possibly exist, we hear you cry. Oh yes, it does, as the following story will show. Let this be a salutary lesson to you:

A family historian had been working for a long time on his branch of the family, which was a fairly unusual name. He had been diligent and efficient, and had built up a substantial family tree. At one point, however, he had hit his 'brick wall' regarding one individual on his tree, and had been stuck for quite a long time, being unable to locate this person's parents. Then one day, when he picked up his research again for further thought, he came up with a brilliant, but complex, idea for a new angle which to his great pleasure, paid off, and he was able to discover who the parents were.

A short time later, when on a genealogy forum, he spotted a request for information from a distant cousin (several times removed), who had also come across the same brick wall as our hero. Delighted to help, he contacted this relative, and provided a step by step breakdown of how he had solved the problem. In reply, he received what he afterwards thought was a fairly muted thank you but then heard nothing else.

He had completely dismissed this contact from his mind until about a year later, when by a series of coincidences he had found himself talking to someone who was involved with a women's group and whose job it was to book speakers for their meetings. When hearing his surname, she asked if he was related to the man who had spoken on family history to quite a few meetings around the district she was responsible for. When finding he was related, she went on to relate what a good speaker this man was, and how interesting it was to see how he had created his family tree – including the innovative way he had broken down his brick wall! Further questioning revealed that the distant cousin had not only claimed this work as his own, but was also earning money as a speaker in part on the back of it.

"Let me assure you, Mr Bund*, where you are going, you will not be able to tell anyone that you are my second cousin once-removed."

*No plagiarism here, of course.

Whilst this is not a true story, however, we have experienced something of this nature that left a nasty taste. Of course, lots of family historians are friendly and helpful and will willingly share what they know with you and also will acknowledge any contribution you make towards their researches. Collaborations can be formed which are rewarding and useful and we would not like to put you off sharing with others. You may need to play the long game - it can be years before any help you give to someone is returned in kind, but family historians tend to have long memories.

You may have been in the position where you have spent hours pulling together information for someone, only for them to never even acknowledge receipt of this, let alone say thank you. There are even cases when entire databases have been given to someone, only to have the same database published on the Internet the very next day by the recipient as if it was their own work.

Not only is the above extremely annoying, but it is also a potential security risk. Allowing someone access to a database that contains personal information about living relatives without their consent is a breach of confidentiality and possibly illegal. Also information such as a person's age, address, occupation and birth details (such as mother's maiden name) could be used by someone for identity fraud. You have a duty of care to the people on whom you hold data and if they have trusted you with such information, it is wrong to pass it on without their knowledge or agreement. Even if the recipient of such information is basically honest, they might forward this information to others when responding to enquiries. If nothing else, they may tack on their own research to yours, which may be incorrect and mislead others.

Kate's comment: *If you receive a request for information from someone, you could initially send them a 'cut down' version of your research, only including items that they could obtain by themselves from public sources. You could miss out any details on living relatives, or information you may have received from privately held sources such as diaries and letters until you feel in a position to trust that person.*

Plagiarism has probably been around since writing was first developed. It was probably a bit more difficult to carry off if the written communication was by way of stone hieroglyphics, but nowadays it is all too easy to do. By way of response, some originators of works have used various devices to detect when their work has been copied. For instance, cartographers have on occasions have inserted 'trap streets' into their maps. These were fictitious places or roads, which if found elsewhere, would point to the map having been copied. One suspected recent example was a fictitious place called Argleton, adjacent to the A59 in Lancashire, which appeared on Google maps in 2009.

This planting of false information is sometimes known as a 'Mountweazel', named after Lillian Virginia Mountweazel, a fountain designer turned photographer. Her very existence was a complete work of fiction, but entered into an encyclopaedia to spot potential theft of information. So if you are serious about avoiding having your own work plagiarised, you could insert your very own Mountweazel into your family tree – not that we are condoning the spreading of even more spurious family history data. But what a temptation it would be to invent a character such as a Great Uncle Hector, whose life was tragically cut short, after drowning in a barrel of decomposing herrings whilst carrying out his life's study of Icelandic lichen. An untimely geyser eruption had caught him unawares and had projected him head down into the said barrel. Although maybe some readers would think there was something a bit fishy about it.....

Trap 45. Your family was dull

When you first introduce the idea to other family members that you wish to share your family history with them, you might need to consider how you manage their expectations. They could well be fantasizing about ancestral highway robbers, inventors, or titled families, but you know that they were all agricultural labourers. Where your family imagine exotic origins, the reality is that they never moved from the village they were born in, and all you have on them is census, birth, marriage and death records. Your ancestors are so dull, the only information of interest you can find is that one once managed to be awarded 2nd place in a biggest marrow contest. Not a hint of bigamy, imbecility or grave-robbing to their names. Some families just seem to keep their noses clean (or never get caught). This probably means that they were honest, sober and hard working - but how can you present such a family in an interesting way?

It can be quite difficult to put a bit of flesh on the bare bones of your family history, without the benefit of the odd murderer or sheep rustler to liven it up. We have previously discussed how we can expand upon our ancestor's lives, including general details about them, the places they lived, their occupations and other things that would have impacted upon them. But what else can we do to 'sex up' an ordinary family?

Whatever you produce to share your family history, this will be more interesting to others if it is visually attractive with illustrations to add a bit of variety and colour, with well-spaced text to make it easy to read. Blocks of text can be broken up with photographs or images relevant to that text. You don't have to put in, say, whole census images but could just extract the bit that refers to your family. You could include extracts from family letters, diaries and invitations to past family celebrations. Have any possessions been handed down to you, even an old tool or button box, which you can find out about and link to an individual in the text? Although you cannot include the items themselves, you could incorporate pictures of them.

If they were from a village you might be able to find out about the history of the village and its population; the type of industries that thrived and the facilities that were available at the time such as pubs, clubs and sporting activities. Include pictures of their town or village, local churches, and schools and link your narrative to them.

It is easy to imagine that our ancestors suffered a life of long working hours, drudgery and servitude with little time for relaxation or fun, but this wasn't always the case. No one worked all day, every day, and holidays existed, even if it was only a few days a year. People did other things, such as Sunday school outings to the seaside, or enjoyed the circus when it came to town. Even if you don't have family photographs or evidence of your family attending, there is a good chance they did and you may be able to get photographs of these events to add colour to your narrative.

Other things you can use to illustrate your story are any little snippets you have collected on the way. If it had been your ancestor who had the aforementioned prize-winning vegetable, include the newspaper clipping that brought this momentous event to your attention, along with a photograph of a large marrow! A bit of comedy can help make a dull story more enjoyable.

If the narrative is a bit thin, you can consider introducing information about what they may have earned, what their daily lives would have been like and the hours they would have worked. History books can shed light on the conditions they might have worked under. You may have found out information like this about their lives but can you interpret it for the reader, such as did their jobs change to reflect changes in the economic climate? How old were the children when they went to work? Did the coming of the railway to their town impact on them? You might not think it very interesting if your ancestor who lived in Camden made backing panels for pianos - until you discover that the piano making industry flourished in that area in the mid to late 1800s because of the proximity to the canal network - and how else are you going to deliver a new piano anywhere in the country cheaply at that time, if not by canal?

Information on the derivation of the relevant surname(s) can be very interesting, and if you include this it is also possible to find maps which show the distribution of these names throughout the country for a couple of time periods, for example, 1881 and 1998. These show not just where incidences of that surname were concentrated in 1881 but also how this has changed after more than one hundred years.

Toni's tip: *Think widely about the lives of your ancestors. For example, if someone ended up in the workhouse, include pictures and information about the place. What would they have eaten, what would have been their routine? There may be contemporary newspaper reports about the place and many workhouses have had their histories compiled - a straightforward Internet search should reveal lots of information for you.*

If all else fails then look sideways - rather than looking into just the direct line, try the side branches of your tree. Someone must surely have done something interesting, unusual or unsavoury, or so you would think.

There is a popular television programme that looks at the family history of selected celebrities. One well-known chat show host was asked to take part in the programme, but despite his doubts that his family had not been interesting, the television company were adamant that they would be able to find something. After six weeks, they came back, defeated. Not one single item worthy of broadcast was found. Does he officially have the most boring family ever?

Trap 46. Your presentation leaves them confused

Presenting your family history could be compared with the delights of assembling flat-packed furniture - inevitably bits are missing and the finished result is never quite how you had imagined. Usually you will have included information about both your direct ancestors and their families, so that you are going both vertically, horizontally and diagonally across the generations, which can be very confusing. This is made worse when each generation re-uses names, so when you are talking about Frederick George and there are seven of them in your tree, you may start to lose the goodwill of your audience.

When presented with a family tree, the tendency is to go straight to the top - to the earliest ancestor - but this might not be the best way to inspire your reader. The people at the top of the tree are usually the ones you know the least about, and there is no law that states you have to start with these people. You could start instead with the current generation and work your way back. By doing this not only do you begin with people who are known to your audience but also brings you more quickly to any juicy bits of family history you may have. The important thing is to present your information in a logical sequence - if you dot around through the generations this leads to confusion. Deal with one family group at a time, although of course there will be some overlapping of the groups, so don't be afraid of including a summary or a relevant section of the family tree at each stage.

If you start with the entire family tree at the beginning of your book or folder in a way that makes it easy to be referred to, such as a loose-leaf insert, or with a spare freestanding copy, this helps the reader pinpoint who is being written about. If you do not have the time to produce a great literary work, then just having the combination of the family tree plus a report generated from your family history database can be very useful. You could consider presenting your work in a half-and-half format, that is, with the history of the family told in narrative form at the front of your presentation with any supporting evidence at the back.

Any evidence you wish to include in your book or folder to corroborate your findings will add to the interest, but only if the reader knows what he is looking at. Any such evidence needs to be clearly titled and dated, with an explanation to help the reader understand each group of records. Just because we as family historians know what a census record looks like and what information is contained therein, this does not mean that a newcomer to the hobby is automatically going to understand what it is all about.

If you are lucky enough to have a comprehensive photographic record of your family, then you could consider a family tree format that allows the inclusion of a thumbnail photograph against each individual on that tree. The same photographs could be used with the narrative to provide a visual clue to the person being talked about.

It can be of great benefit to spare an hour or two to talk through your findings with any interested party. This gives them a chance to ask questions and clarify items they are not sure of. This also has the benefit of giving you immediate feedback and the chance to tease out other interesting family information, as this process can often trigger new memories.

Toni's tip: Get other relatives to write their memories of family members or specific events and include these in your written account. This will add interest and reduce the amount of work you have to do yourself - but don't forget to credit them for this work.

Trap 47. You have bad news to break

In an earlier section we have dealt with how to cope when your ancestors turn out to be the most boring people on earth. Now we need to deal with the opposite end of the spectrum - what if they are too interesting? Supposing you have found evidence that in your family is a person who has been 'up before the beak' for a range of crimes such as bigamy, slander, breach of the peace, inciting assault, fraud, debt, and brothel-keeping - and they are only a couple of generations away.

There is a lot of pleasure to be derived from the more unusual things we discover, and you can get quite a buzz from uncovering a bigamist or murderer in the family. We can enjoy finding these things because the people involved are long gone and we didn't actually know them. It adds colour to our background but we are safe in the knowledge that our genes have been diluted and shuffled around in the subsequent generations and so it is unlikely that our sons have inherited the tendency to poison their parents (we hope).

Where it does start to get difficult is when the events you uncover are closer to home. Just how might Great Aunt Margaret react to the news that her parents had lied about their date of marriage, to cover the fact that her older sister was born one month after the true marriage date? She might be horrified to find out that her parents were not as innocent as they seemed; conversely, she might find it uproariously funny. So do you tell her, or not?

> **Kate's comment:** *We had a big secret in our family. My father remembers fondly his grandfather - his father's father - as a kindly old man who would walk him to the cake shop when he was young to buy him a custard slice (his favourite). However, when I was researching this side of the family, I found that this nice old man was not in fact my dad's grandfather, but his great-grandfather. He and his wife had brought up my grandfather as their own child, but in fact he was the illegitimate son of their eldest daughter (father unknown). I was then left with the tricky subject of how to tell my father that his dad had been born illegitimate and that the person he had thought of as his granddad was his great-granddad. Dad had no idea this was the case and it is quite possible that my grandfather did not know, either.*

Our work in discovering other people's roots has meant that from time to time we have uncovered all kinds of skeletons in the cupboard. On one occasion we found a convicted child murderer, who was hung at Newgate Gaol. Fortunately he was not in the direct line, but the brother of the direct ancestor. Another time, we found that someone's father had been married twice, and had three children by his first marriage, about which the client was totally unaware. This meant that we had discovered that he had three half-siblings, which was not an easy thing to break to him.

The most difficult piece of news to break, however, was when a client wanted his family history researched and therefore had provided details of his birth, his parents and his grandparents. As a matter of routine, however, these details were checked and unfortunately despite extremely thorough searching, no record of his birth could be found in the General Register Office indexes. At our request, he provided a copy of his birth certificate, which was a short form, not a full certificate. The wording on this certificate showed us what the problem was.

A standard short form certificate has the words *"The above particulars have been compiled from an entry in my custody"* at the end of the document. His certificate stated *"Certified to have been compiled from the records in the custody of the Registrar General Office."* This wording means only one thing - he had been adopted. So this presented us with a huge dilemma - to tell or not to tell. We could either say we couldn't do the work and give him back his fee, or simply tell the truth - and did we have the right to do that? After much discussion, we decided that Toni would talk to his wife and ask her advice.

"I am afraid it is true, Mr Hopkins. Your family are in fact from Tunbridge Wells."

When you set off to uncover your family history it is generally with a sense of fun and intrigue, and for most people the last thing you would expect would be to have the rug pulled so thoroughly from under your feet. Finding such secrets can make people feel that they no longer know who they are.

Another client approached us because he had an unusual surname of which he was quite proud and he wanted to know a bit more about its origins. During the course of the research it was discovered that just a couple of generations back, the direct ancestor and his siblings had been informally adopted by their mother's new partner and had taken on his unusual surname. Their actual birth name was one which appears in the list of the 20 most frequently occurring surnames in the UK. Had this situation not occurred, this would have been the surname our client would have had, and genetically he had no claim whatsoever on the unusual surname he used. He later told us that he had been deeply affected by this turn of events and it had made him feel like a different person.

Trap 48. You get carried away

The Americans earned worldwide censure for the cruel and unusual torture method they used on the inmates at Guantanamo prison. They played music, including the "I Love You" song from the children's TV show 'Barney.' What would have been far more subtle yet effective would have been to import some genealogists to tell the captives all about their family history research findings. It is very easy to become a family history bore, as it is a hobby that can completely take over your life if you let it. Unless you have a partner who is equally obsessive, there is a good chance that the hobby can have an adverse impact on your relationship. When it gets to the point when your partner puts your photograph on the children's bedroom wall with a sign saying 'This is what your mother/father looks like,' then you know it has too firm a grip on you.

So what level of obsession are you at? Read the list below and decide which one is the most accurate description of you:

Level 1 (mild): You occasionally pick up a Family History magazine from the Newsagent's when you are passing. You can find your way around BMD sites and you like to watch celebrity family history programmes on the television. You are still able to show interest in other things and remember the birthdays of living members of your family.

Level 2 (intermediate): You subscribe to at least two Family History magazines and at least one on-line genealogy website; you encourage your family to spend holidays near to the record office you want to visit; you know off by heart the dates of the UK census and when Civil Registration first started; you asked for and received a scanner/photocopier for your last birthday; and you get irritated with the cat when she sits on the census printout you just made.

Level 3 (dangerous): Redecoration becomes immaterial because your walls are covered with family trees; personal grooming starts to slip; you feel you now know more than the 'experts' in the family history magazines; at (increasingly rare) social occasions, no one wants to sit next to you; you forget to feed the cat for three days then give it five tins of Kittiemunchie in one go.

Level 4 (certifiable): Eating, drinking and sleeping become annoying diversions from your true life's work; the money you have saved by no longer visiting the hairdresser can be spent on a microfiche reader; most times you feel you are actually living in the past; you feed your children gruel and threaten to send them to the workhouse; you don't notice the cat has moved in with the next-door-neighbour and your partner is thinking about doing the same.

Hopefully you will hover around the level 1 or 2 mark, as if you are at a 3 or 4 then frankly there is little hope for you. What you can try to do is to incorporate ordinary family things into your obsession so that you still manage to communicate with your nearest and dearest, and may even manage to get them interested and involved. You could, for instance, organise a trip to the town where your grandmother was born. There, you can take your family shopping, have a picnic, enjoy the sights and have a game of 'who can be first to spot our surname on a grave' in the local cemetery. This may work a few times before they wise up to it.

> *Toni's tip:* Children are never going to be interested in dry facts like dates of birth or places of baptism. You might be able to engage their interest more with tales of what their ancestors did for a living. If your great grandfather had been a coal miner, try taking them to a mine that is open for visitors (such as the National Mining Museum of Wales) so they can get a flavour of what life would have been like for him.

Others have struggled with this idea of getting their family members interested in their hobby. Recently there have been family history books written with the aim of getting children on board. More unusually, a well known UK family history magazine formed a partnership with a very well known Japanese 'virtual pet' manufacturer to provide an on-line facility for children to produce fantasy family trees for their virtual pet. Not sure whether as children it would have worked for us, though.

Trap 49. Your research dies with you

Sometimes, we just have a driving need to leave something of ourselves to the world after we have departed it. Egyptian pharaohs built massive pyramids to house their mortal remains and remind the world of how truly great they were. The American pioneer Johnny Appleseed reputedly planted orchards wherever he went. The British nobility did it in a more eccentric fashion by building grand follies on their estates.

Unless you are in possession of great wealth, large numbers of slaves, vast estates or a lot of apple tree saplings, none of the above methods are going to be available for you to make your mark on history. What you do own, however, is a collection of papers relating to your family history research and these can be the basis of your legacy to coming generations. You need to think seriously about what is going to happen to your researches, as you do not want to run the risk of it all being thrown away in the event of your demise or loss of marbles.

This may not be an issue if you know of someone in your family who shares your passion and to whom you can entrust your documentation. Even if there is no one immediately obvious who could take this on, it should be possible to find a family member who could be entrusted with your researches until such time as a new genealogist arrives to take up the baton of responsibility.

What you will need to consider is how you are going to 'future-proof' your researches. No matter how up to date you are with developments in electronics, computing and other media, we have no way of telling how things are going to be done in years to come. What we may think is 'cutting edge' now, could be the source of hilarity or bafflement in 40, 30 or even 20 year's time. How many of you can remember, let alone still use, 8-track music players; Betamax video players, or laser discs . . .

"Does anyone know how this book thing works?"

To make the analogy, just imagine if your Great-Uncle Robert dies and his widow knows you are interested in family history. Robert was an amateur genealogist and therefore you are the natural successor to him. Solemnly, you are presented with his life's work, on a set of 5.25 inch floppy disks. So not only is it going to cost you a fair bit to get these converted to a CD format but in any case there is no guarantee that whatever software packages he used could be accessed easily in any useable form today. Yet when Robert made these disks he was utilising the most modern technology available at the time.

> **Toni's tip:** *I have arranged for my son to be custodian of my research. He has agreed to try to make sure it always stays current to reflect any changes in media and format.*

Whatever media you use to store your researches in at present, this information is likely to degrade over time - it is just a question of how much time. We do not know what it will be replaced with - possibly a microchip imbedded into your brain? Before you book your brain surgery, perhaps you should think about storing your information in more than one format so you have more than one chance of it being accessible in the future.

You could start by converting everything you have at present into the most up to date format, i.e. scan all photographs, certificates and documents into digital images and store them as both pdf and jpeg files. You can also save your word-processed documents into one of these image formats too, as over time, word-processing packages can change dramatically. Slides, home movies and tape recordings can all be transferred to digital formats. Databases can also be saved in more than one format - you may be able to save into a gedcom version or a .csv format. Family trees can generally be saved as a pdf version.

Once you have built up an electronic 'library' of all your information, you can then store this in more than one format, e.g. on CD and DVD, flash drives or external hard drives. You could consider storing a copy on a storage website but this of course is only as good and long-lasting as the company running the website.

As we have said before, your original documentation is best kept on acid free paper and in special wallets. However, there is always the possibility that technology may not be the way forward - if we are prey to the doom-monger predictions of volcanoes, meteorite impacts, nuclear wars, floods, droughts, epidemics and the death of bees, we might as a result have technology no more advanced than banging rocks together. In which case, just to be on the safe side, you might also like to develop a version of your family history that can be interpreted through the medium of song and dance.

Trap 50. Expect the unexpected

The chances of winning the lottery are not that high. Imagine winning the lottery jackpot twice using the same numbers. It is estimated to be around 5 trillion to 1; so you would never, ever, expect it to happen, it is just too unlikely. So imagine the surprise of the Hampshire man when his numbers came up for the second time. This just illustrates that even the most astonishing things can happen, and this is also true of your family history. On occasions you will get something that is not just unexpected, but is the equivalent of a genealogical googly, when every stone you turn uncovers something more and more unbelievable. Plus this is such a good (and true) story that we just had to share it with you.

Our story is a tale of star-crossed lovers, poor Celia and her young beau, John. Celia was born in Ardingly, West Sussex, around 1800. Celia did not grow properly and in adulthood reached her maximum height of 4ft 3ins. It is speculated that she had a form of dwarfism as she had many of the physical symptoms shown by people with those types of genetic abnormalities.

At the age of around 24, Celia found the man of her dreams. He was the 18-year old John Holloway, who at 5ft 2ins was also a tad on the short side but to her, he was just perfect. They became lovers, although it could be said that for Celia, loved burned more brightly than for John, as he allegedly felt awkward being seen in public with her because of her slightly unusual appearance, so he courted her mainly by night.

John and Celia went to live in Brighton, and Celia became pregnant. John refused to make an honest woman of her, so in distress she returned to Ardingly and appealed for help from the Parish authorities. Life for a single, pregnant dwarf in the 1820's was not going to be easy. They sympathised with her predicament and called for Holloway's arrest. He was dragged to Lewes prison and incarcerated there – holding out for five weeks before reluctantly agreeing to make Celia his wife. They were married in Ardingly but then the Overseers of the Poor ordered them to leave the village. They made their way back to Brighton, taking up residence in the Elm Grove Workhouse. No doubt John was feeling trapped in a loveless marriage, and to make matters worse, the reason for that marriage – their child – was stillborn. John started drinking heavily and knocking Celia about. Eventually he left to join the Naval Blockade Service in Rye.

Whilst serving in Rye, John met and fell in love with another woman, Ann. Fairly soon she became pregnant and appealed to the Rye Overseers for help, who visited John to sort out the problem. Not fancying another spell of porridge, John claimed to be single and married Ann bigamously.

John left the Naval Blockade service in 1829 and got work on the Chain Pier, which was undergoing construction. He then hatched his diabolical plan for Celia. By this time, Celia was living with friends in Brighton. John visited her, and expressed remorse for their former animosities and begged her to live with him again. Celia still carried a torch for her man and so agreed to go with him to the lodgings he had secured. He first came and got all her belongings. Celia must have had a few doubts as she expressed concerns that he might hop it with her stuff and never be seen again, but true to his word he turned up later to take her to their new home.

She was not seen again until August 1831, when two farm labourers spotted a piece of red cloth poking out of what looked like disturbed earth. A body was found, although contemporary descriptions state that "… the head and the arms were wanting". The dismembered body was declared to be Celia's remains by a Mrs Bishop, wife of a farm labourer and Celia's sister.

John was arrested and confessed to the murder. He had strangled poor Celia, and together with Ann, disposed of the body. The head was put in a cupboard and the arms thrown down a privy. The remaining body parts were transported in a trunk to the somewhat inaptly named Lovers Walk, where John buried them.

John was sentenced to be hanged. On his execution day, he gave a speech to the crowd saying he suffered justly and that he had spilt innocent blood. Throwing himself to God's mercy, he stepped onto the platform and the drop fell. It was said that the struggles of the culprit continued for some minutes.

So you have now reached the end of our book and if you are still keen on researching your family history - well, you have been warned. We, the authors, cannot be held responsible for the presence of dwarf-stranglers or other undesirables in your ancestry! The best advice we can offer is to be careful who you run off to Brighton with, especially if you are exceptionally short.

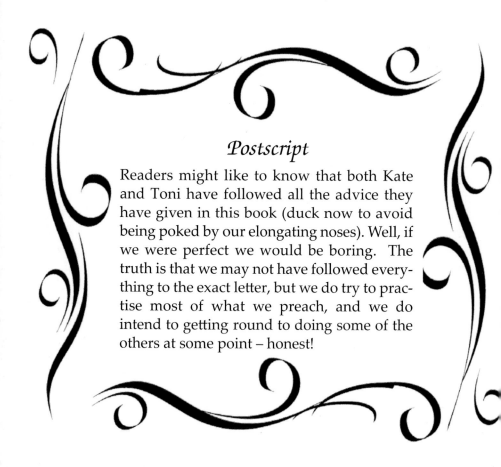

Postscript

Readers might like to know that both Kate and Toni have followed all the advice they have given in this book (duck now to avoid being poked by our elongating noses). Well, if we were perfect we would be boring. The truth is that we may not have followed everything to the exact letter, but we do try to practise most of what we preach, and we do intend to getting round to doing some of the others at some point – honest!